RETHINK
HAPPINESS

"For years now I've witnessed the transforming impact of Paul George at our Steubenville Conferences. His ability to deliver an engaging and relevant message is unparalleled."

Mark Joseph
Franciscan University of Steubenville

"Paul George is an extraordinary storyteller. His writing style is like sitting down with a trusted friend and having an engaging conversation that leaves you wanting to know what happens next. In *Rethink Happiness*, Paul shares delightful stories about his search for genuine happiness and his missteps along the way. He also invites us into intimate conversation with people he has accompanied in their pursuit of lasting fulfillment. The stories are real and engaging and potentially life-changing. There is profound wisdom in this unassuming book. I highly recommend it to anyone who is longing for greater fulfillment in life. Isn't that all of us?"

Bob Schuchts
Author of *Be Healed*

"Paul's ministry has positively impacted millions of young people around the world. He has a unique ability to make the Christian life real and transparent in a way that brings hope for us all."

Randy Raus
Life Teen

"Paul George has been a good friend to my family and me for many years since ministering to my NFL teammate's Bible study group at the New Orleans Saints. In *Rethink Happiness*, Paul has a special way of weaving his life experiences with anecdotal humor and relevant scripture. This book leads you to an examination of conscience that is life-giving and transforming. Even the reflection questions at the end of each chapter encourage you to go deeper in your journey with the Lord. Paul vividly paints word pictures so that his experiences come to life, and at times I laughed out loud with his descriptions of monumental moments that make him the amazing speaker and storyteller he is today. My life has been personally changed by my friendship with Paul and all he has offered in sharing his faith journey."

John Carney
Retired kicker for the New Orleans Saints

"In *Rethink Happiness*, Paul George has tapped into the longing of every human heart. In an engaging manner, accessible for all, Paul is able to help us understand our own heart, and at the same time, discover the heart of God. Drawing from his own experience and stories of saints, NFL football players, and hurricanes, Paul engages the reader no matter their life experience, and he shares that happiness is possible. Paul leads each of us in discovering where, or in whom, our heart will find happiness."

Rev. Dave Pivonka, T.O.R.
Author of *Breath of God*

"Everyone desires happiness but no one seems to know where to find it—until now. In *Rethink Happiness*, Paul George doesn't just ask the question everyone asks, he offers the answer few have found. Drawing from timeless wisdom, personal experience and good, old-fashioned common sense, George walks the reader through the minefield of modern thought with sage wisdom and practical guidance. Each page is filled with anecdotal proof that a life of happiness and true joy is not only plausible but possible! A gifted storyteller, Paul George has penned a thought-provoking read here—one that will leave hearts and minds engaged and moved. I loved this book and cannot wait to give it to those closest to me. Life is meant to be lived, not merely survived. This book is an invaluable tool to ensure we never sacrifice the former and settle for the latter."

Mark Hart
Life Teen

"I highly recommend Paul's book. Through the sharing of his personal experiences, Paul provides practical and realistic ways for the ordinary person to grow in one's walk with Christ. Paul is also a gifted speaker, who, through wisdom and life experiences, is able to speak to different audiences effectively."

Most Rev. Sam Jacobs
Bishop emeritus of the Diocese of Houma-Thibodaux

"*Rethink Happiness* offers a profoundly inspired examination of the heart so that we can embrace God's love for us, our purpose, and ultimately, true happiness. Paul George is challenging, honest, and encouraging in helping us become who we were made to be."

Leah Darrow
International speaker and author of *The Other Side of Beauty*

RETHINK
HAPPINESS

DARE TO EMBRACE GOD AND EXPERIENCE TRUE JOY

PAUL GEORGE

Foreword by Matt Maher

AVE MARIA PRESS AVE Notre Dame, Indiana

Founded in 1865, Ave Maria Press is a ministry of the United States Province of Holy Cross.

www.avemariapress.com

Paperback: ISBN-13 978-1-59471-791-8

E-book: ISBN-13 978-1-59471-792-5

Cover images © / ConWeb / Adobe Stock and Color_Brush / iStockphoto.

Cover design by Brianna Dombo.

Text design by Brian C. Conley.

Printed and bound in the United States of America

Library of Congress Cataloging-in-Publication Data is available.

To Jesus:
For giving me purpose and meaning.

To my family:
Gretchen, you are the best decision I ever made (behind my decision for Christ). Marie, Jacob, Sarah, Clare, and Adeline—y'all are the greatest joys of my life. I love you.

To Mom, Dad, and Lulie:
Thank you.

To Bishop Sam Jacobs:
Thank you for journeying with me, for being Christ to me, even when I was far away, and for teaching me what it means to truly live.

For happiness is that perfect good which entirely satisfies one's desire; otherwise it would not be the ultimate end, if something yet remained to be desired.

–St. Thomas Aquinas

CONTENTS

FOREWORD

They say you get to choose your friends, and while I don't necessarily disagree with that maxim, I don't think it gives the whole picture. There are some friendships in life that seem scripted and set by the hand of God.

When I was twenty-three years old, I was a newly "born-again" Catholic, finishing a music degree at Arizona State University and working part-time at a Catholic parish in Mesa, Arizona. It was 1997. That summer, I met Paul George, who was recently hired as the new youth minister at the parish where I worked. I remember the first time we met for coffee—he, the obvious former college athlete, and me, the slacker cigarette-smoking musician with long hair. We were an unlikely pair. I immediately had a sense that (1) he was more mature than I was, (2) that wasn't saying much, and (3) he actually knew the Bible.

That fall, at Paul's request, I led worship for the first time for a Bible study of thirty-five kids on a Monday night. Over the next decade, a friendship formed on a foundation of knowing and believing in a God who continues to have life-changing encounters with people. On every occasion that we ministered together—from small Bible studies and youth group nights to conferences with youth pastors and conferences and worship nights with thousands of young people—I was ministered to by the words, perspective, and thoughts of Paul George. Paul would close every Sunday night youth group talk with a Bible in his hand, authentically sharing his love, passion, and faith for Jesus with anyone who had ears to hear; and almost every youth night would end the same way—with Paul calling people to conversion.

Paul has a unique vocation to specifically call folks to conversion while communicating the Gospel. That might seem redundant, but too often in the Christian life, we think of conversion as a singular event and not a process—as something that happened, not something that happened and is still happening. Paul sees clearly that conversion is a process. After ten years of involvement in local Church ministry, he and I found ourselves on a tour bus traveling together to different cities around America to hold worship nights—me leading worship and Paul still consistently calling people to a different way of looking at life.

With this book, *Rethink Happiness*, Paul is still doing that same thing: inviting people to look at the call to conversion in their lives and to respond.

During those Sunday night youth group talks by Paul, I always sensed that it wasn't just the teens who benefited. All the adult volunteers in the room were being ministered to as well. I never left Sunday night without feeling convicted about some aspect of my life. Whether it was my ambitions, my motivations, or my desires, I was always in a place of being consoled or being convicted. I remember the kids lining up to talk to him privately afterward. They knew he had a genuine concern for them and their lives. I know how life-changing Paul's presence and gifts were for so many people.

With *Rethink Happiness*, you're getting your own personal time with Paul. I encourage you to go slowly with this book. Rather than just read it from start to finish, let each chapter be a separate conversion that starts an interior conversation, one that can continue as long as it needs to, and when you're ready, you can move on to the next one. Let the questions at the end of each chapter launch you into the unknown spaces of your own heart. To quote the most-used phrase in the Bible, "Do not be afraid!"

More than ever, people today need to be met with the Good News of a God who loves them completely just as they are. With this book, Paul is doing what he was made to do. My hope and prayer for you is that you, too, can take time to pause and make yourself available to our Lord, who calls you to new horizons.

Matt Maher

INTRODUCTION

An enormous portion of my childhood was spent on a sports team of some kind—I was a multisport athlete for many years, excelling at whatever I played. By the time I reached my junior year in high school, playing sports in college was a real possibility. I wavered between playing football, baseball, or both in college. Baseball eventually won out, and I had a blast playing the sport I loved. I had worked hard, dreamed big, and practiced intensely enough to be in the running to play professional ball one day.

But in late spring of my senior year in college, I found myself sitting on the edge of a hospital bed. I had suffered a debilitating shoulder injury that would forever change the trajectory of my life. I remember sitting there, staring into space, unable to focus on anything the doctor was saying to me. The more the doctor talked, the further I faded, wishing this wasn't real. The reality of the news was setting in: I would never play sports again. My hopes, my dreams, and my plans were coming to a screeching halt. As I lay in bed after the doctor left, my mind wandered. Everything seemed to be crashing in at once—not just the news from the doctor but many other parts of my life, too (which I will share in this book). My life wasn't what I wished or hoped it would become, and truth be told, I wasn't fulfilled. I didn't even know where to start looking for happiness.

Although I don't know you, we probably have a lot in common. For starters, we both want to be happy. We both desire to have peace in the midst of life's storms. We both need to love authentically and to be authentically loved. We both crave true, lasting happiness. I can't promise a quick fix to your struggles, but I can offer you some food for thought as you begin to unpack your own experiences and define who you are. But before we can successfully reach any new territory, you'll need to recognize that this takes not only effort but also time. You see, life is a journey, and although we may experience life-altering events that change us overnight, for the most part, true change happens slowly over time. In Christian circles, we call this lasting change, which naturally involves turning our hearts and minds to God, *conversion.*

The Greek root of the word *conversion* means "to rethink."

Rethink what? Rethink the way we live. Rethink who we are. Rethink our purpose. Rethinking life allows us to transform into the person God created us to be.

When we consider our lives through the lens of God's design for us, the process of true conversion begins. We start this process when we stop looking at our lives through the lenses of the world, others' opinions of us, and even our own negative thoughts about ourselves. Thankfully, the new life we desire and the happiness we seek are available to each one of us. We only need to say yes.

In my own life's journey and the many challenges I'll share throughout this book, I've tasted both counterfeit and authentic happiness. And I can attest to the fact that once you taste authentic happiness, you know it's real, sweet, and lasting. I hope that as you read this book, you will discover (or rediscover) this gift from God.

This book isn't a twelve-step guide to happiness or a quick fix for life's problems. We are not made simply to be "fixed" or "solved." We are created for much more. This book is meant to be your companion as you tackle some of the most important questions you'll ever ask yourself—as you begin to *rethink* what really matters to *you*. You might begin by asking for the first (or fiftieth!) time what you really want out of life, what you imagine to be God's role in your desires, how you've been treating yourself and your deepest wishes, and why you might struggle to accept God's gift of authentic happiness.

I suggest that you start by telling yourself that you are *made to thrive* and to be happy. You want this, and God wills it for you. Happiness might not look like what the world tries to sell to you, and it's probably not what you've spent most of your resources pursuing. But I assure you that when you begin honoring yourself as a child of God and stop pursuing the wrong goals, a deep peace and joy will overcome you. Together, in the following pages, we will dissect life and find out how we can find fulfillment even in the midst of all its complexities. We will uncover, discover, and unfold the author of happiness, Christ himself.

Do not hesitate to move through this book slowly. Read sections and then sit with them for a while. Allow yourself to really digest the questions that come at the end of each chapter. Challenge your assumptions about God, yourself, and your notion of happiness. When you feel hesitant or afraid, that's the time to dig in. Ask yourself why you feel this way and where it's coming from. Only digging deep and applying brutal honesty can lead to the authentic happiness you're really looking for.

Like you, I long for authentic happiness and desire it more than anything else. I hope this book helps you *rethink* your life and examine the decisions you've made, are making, and plan to make. I hope the stories I share about myself and the people I've worked with inspire you to think beyond skin-deep and into who you are and what God intends for you.

Different circumstances wake us up to the reality of God. For me it was lying on a hospital bed. What's your circumstance? What questions are you asking about life?

It's your turn. Let's wake up your heart, your mind, your soul to true happiness. Let's rethink everything you've ever assumed about happiness and your destiny. You were created to thrive in this life. So let's get started.

CHAPTER 1

WE ARE ALL STARVING

As a teenager, I lived in the country outside of a small town. Usually the twenty-minute drive home on the quiet two-lane road was uneventful, relaxing, and reflective. But on one particular late night I was driving fast. My old, small, four-cylinder truck was barreling down the highway at ninety-five miles an hour. I turned off my headlights and the road became pitch black. I began to drive through the curves of the road, hugging each turn like a NASCAR driver. My intention wasn't to prove that I was a good driver—my intention was to eventually fly off the side of the road.

I had reached a place where I felt as if my life had no purpose. "What's the point of living?" I wondered. I could blame that moment on a bad breakup, the loss of an important football game, low grades, loneliness, confusion, doubt, fear, or issues at home, but it wasn't just one of those things; it was the culmination of them all weighing on me simultaneously.

Hugging the edge of the road near the ditch, I could feel the gravel beneath my tires. All I had to do was let go of the steering wheel and my truck would take me to a place where none of those things would burden me any longer. Although it was dark that night and my headlights were turned off, the reflection of the moon cast a faint light in the night sky, on the road in front of me, and on the rows of soybeans on each side.

In the midst of the darkness there was a gleam of light that kept me from letting go. The small amount of light from the sun reflected by the moon was all I needed to see ahead. I got scared and pulled my truck farther onto the road and turned my headlights back on. I wasn't so much afraid to die as I was afraid for my life to end before I found the answers. I knew there had to be more in life, and I had a strong desire to discover what it was.

In that moment, that faint reflection of light was all I needed. It represented a small glimmer of hope inside me that wanted to find meaning. I know now that hope was God. Hope kept me from giving up and led me on a search for the answers I was seeking. Hope can be a small but powerful thing, and it was hope that kept me alive that night.

When I look back, I'm certain that God had his hand on my life.

I eventually made it home. As I lay in bed that night, my heart still pounded and my mind was spinning with thoughts. I began to ask questions directed at an unknown God. I asked why I was still alive and what my purpose was.

The reality is that, despite these moments of questioning the value of my own existence, I was blessed with a wonderful mother and father. I'm honored to have a close relationship with both of them today. However, our life wasn't easy. Like many families, we faced challenges. My parents divorced when I was eight years old, and it was hard on all of us. Many years later, my mom, dad, sister, and I all acknowledged the trials we went through, but we also saw that God did good things through our hardship.

After the divorce, like many kids, I found myself confused about who I was. I was confused about the meaning of life. I was confused about why I existed. I was confused about God and wondered how he could allow life to be so difficult. I was angry, frustrated, and disappointed that life wasn't ideal. My worldview changed. I rebelled and withdrew from those who loved me most, and I sought comfort in things that didn't love me at all.

I was exposed early to the reality that eventually hits us all—that life is hard, imperfect, and not what we want it to be. I decided that I needed to live life alone, so I closed my heart to others, and I closed my soul to God. The only thing I expected out of life was disappointment.

Oh, I had happy moments and have happy memories, but they were sandwiched between confusion and mistakes, seeking and not finding, fear and doubt.

You and I may go about our search in different ways, but for all of us, the desire for authentic joy is paramount. As much as our bodies desire to breathe, so do our souls long for happiness, and none of us are void of this desire.

I've traveled the planet and met people from all over the world, and it's interesting to discover that what I long for is the same thing someone from another continent wants as well. Why is this? It's because the desire for fulfillment runs deep into our very nature, and we will never be truly happy until we satisfy it. Written into our hearts is a desire, craving, and longing for fulfillment. We want meaning and a purpose in life.

Jesus offers us the answers to our deepest questions. He says, "I am the way, and the truth, and the life" (Jn 14:6). Christ offers us a new way of living. Through him—the way, the truth, and the life—is the way to true fulfillment.

St. Augustine said, "Where then are these rules written, if not in the book of that light we call the truth? In it is written every just law; from it the law passes into the heart of the man who does justice, not that it migrates into it, but that it places its imprint on it, like a seal on a ring that passes onto wax, without leaving the ring" (quoted in *CCC*, 1955). St. Augustine was a man who wandered for years in search for meaning. Yet his search wasn't far away. It was woven in his heart and soul—the place where God writes his love and truth in all of us. Augustine speaks of God's nature not only from a theological perspective but also from a personal conversion—an encounter with the Savior. Jesus.

St. Thomas Aquinas framed it this way: "The natural law is nothing other than the light of understanding placed in us by God; through it we know what we must do and what we must avoid. God has given this light or law at the creation" (quoted in *CCC*, 1955). The desire of our heart, who we are as humans, draws us to discover our purpose.

I've never starved, but there have been times when I've been really hungry. I'm sure you have as well, right? Well, my grandmother always said, "The key to good cooking is waiting till people are really hungry, and then they'll eat just about anything and think it's good." When I'm really hungry, everything seems to taste good.

One night when I was working late, the phone rang around midnight. I answered it quickly, assuming some sort of emergency was the reason for the call. On the other end was my friend Josh, and I could hear his radio blaring eighties music in the background. I asked him what he was doing, and he said that ever since his wife became pregnant, he made late-night runs to a local fast-food joint to buy her jumbo cups of ice. I asked him if they had an ice machine at their house and he said yes, but she craved this specific type of ice. He knew this because once he tried to disguise a different type of ice and got caught; apparently this was the only ice that satisfied her craving.

Our bodies were created to crave what they need, and not only during pregnancy. These cravings give us an appetite that leads us to find food. When our appetites are triggered by some complex movement of the hormonal system, we crave; and when we crave, we eat; and when we eat, our hunger is satisfied. This process goes on throughout our lives, and most of the time we don't even think about it. Without craving and the urge to eat, we would starve and eventually die.

We may need to be taught what to eat or how to eat, but the simple urge to eat is already there, and our bodies obey it.

Just as we crave food, we also have emotional and spiritual cravings. We crave things such as attention, love, fame, money, success, happiness, fulfillment, and so on. All of our cravings long to be satisfied.

This search to satisfy my cravings was a driving force in my life for too long. My insecurities, stemming from not knowing myself, led me to seek immediate fulfillment in things that left me hungrier than before.

I remember hanging out with some older friends in high school who were partying. At age fourteen, I sat on the tailgate of a truck in the middle of a cornfield chugging down whatever alcohol they gave me. I didn't want to drink—I actually thought getting drunk was dumb—but I wanted to be liked more than I wanted *not* to drink. I wanted to fit in more than I wanted *not* to chug cheap liquor. And because I didn't like myself, I didn't think anyone else liked me, and I was willing to do almost anything to feel accepted. I was starving to find my worth. I was thirsty to find meaning.

My "friends" left me there that night, and I remember lying in the field wondering if my life had any meaning. In my search to find myself, I lay in a muddy cornfield with more questions than answers. Who was I, where was God, and was happiness even attainable?

Often we believe that our cravings are what they seem on the surface, but in reality they run deep into our being. We may think one thing will satisfy our cravings, yet once we set our eyes on something bigger and better, we look to that instead.

I once had a conversation with a wealthy CEO, who told me that he had purchased eight cars in a two-week span. I asked him if he needed eight cars. He said no, not really. Then I asked why he went on a sudden shopping spree for something he didn't really need. He said that he thought it would satisfy him.

Most of us can't buy eight cars, but imagine some high-dollar but affordable item you like and consider buying eight of them in two weeks; you start to see where he was coming from. He told me that he would drive one of his new cars for two days and end up feeling the same as before, so he would go out and buy another one. After two weeks, he had the fleet of his dreams, but he said his dreams weren't "being fulfilled." He was still craving more!

I've lost count of the number of conversations I've had with people who follow this pattern and are left in the same position, or worse than they were before. Even more are the conversations I've had with individuals who return to the same things over and over again, hoping that the next time they will get a different result.

A young woman once confessed to me that she couldn't end a bad relationship with a guy she was dating because the emotional and physical intimacy she received in the relationship fed a void in her heart. She filled her craving to be loved with short moments of intimacy from an abusive guy. Her desire to be loved was good and natural, but she chose the wrong thing to satisfy it. Although she had moments of satisfaction, they wore off rapidly, to the point where she wasn't happy at all. Sad and dejected, she was willing to overlook the abuse to have her needs met temporarily—which only caused more pain. Fortunately, she eventually found a way out and now has true fulfillment.

It isn't hard to see the emptiness that lies underneath the surface of our culture. The craving for fame, sex, attention, money, success, and so on only hides what people are really longing for. From a macro view, the world is full of people who are emotionally and spiritually starving. On the micro level, many of my conversations with people center on their malnutrition. What they are feasting on is not only failing to satisfy their deep hunger within but is also actually making them sick. Let's take a look at my acquaintance Walter for an easy example of this phenomenon.

I spend lots of time traveling for work as a speaker, consultant, and life coach. In the process, I've collected many air miles and have developed some habits. On these trips, I spend most of my time meeting with people and trying to be as present and available as possible. There is very little downtime, and I'm OK with that. When I'm on a plane, I either sleep, catch up on writing, send emails, or get completely lost in a book or movie.

However, there are times when someone will engage me in conversation. One time, I was flying to New York City to speak at a conference and fell asleep. I woke up with about forty-five minutes left on the flight. I had just enough time to work on a few things before arriving. But apparently, my co-passenger, Walter, was eager to talk to someone. He had waited for me to wake up and as soon as I did, he asked me a question.

"Are you coming or going?"

"Kind of both," I said. "I'm coming and going."

Silence.

"Where are you going?" he asked.

"New York City," I said, as politely as possible.

Silence.

"What's taking you to NYC?" he asked.

"Work."

My answers were short because I didn't want to chitchat; however, I was cordial and waited to see if he really wanted to talk. He did.

"What do you do?" he asked.

I told him that I'm a speaker and life coach. Now I'm knee-deep in this conversation, and since turnaround is fair play, I began to fire back, asking him all the questions he asked me. Walter was headed to France, and he was traveling alone with the hope of meeting an old girlfriend he rediscovered on the Internet. (They met long before the Internet existed and lost contact.) He was about sixty-five years old with short gray hair, dressed snappy-casual, tanned, and freshly shaven. He had never married, although he had had a few long-term relationships that "never panned out." There was loneliness in his eyes. He shared with me how he had retired at age forty after, as he put it, "getting lucky in the commercial real-estate industry." I was intrigued.

"What have you been doing since forty?" I asked. He said he took up sailing and began traveling around the world by sailboat. He'd seen just about everything in the past twenty-five years.

At this point, I'm not only intrigued but also enthralled by his story. Who doesn't want to retire at forty and travel around the world without a care?

As I immersed myself in Walter's story, I didn't grasp that he was just as intrigued by mine. He dominated me when it came to cash, early retirement, leisurely travel, and a carefree life. Apparently I dominated him when it came to living with purpose, relationships, and faith.

After we told our stories, and there were no more questions, we both went back to what we were doing. I was hoping to finish my work before the plane landed. About five minutes later, I felt a tap on my shoulder. It was Walter, and in an awkward moment he looked at me, his eyes a little watery.

"I've never been this vulnerable with anyone before," he said. I leaned away a little bit but kept eye contact with him, waiting for him to follow up his statement.

"I've been retired for years and have traveled the world by land, air, and sea," he said. "I've seen and experienced everything, yet I can't seem to find the happiness and purpose you speak about. You seem to have found something I want to know more about."

I thought, *How can it be possible for someone with so much to long for so much more?* Then I realized, he's human, and his *heart* longs to be satisfied, just as mine does. Walter continued on to France, but his journey that day led him to find the way, the truth, and the life—Jesus.

We all wish life could be perfect, but it's not. And if it was, we would still search for meaning until we found it. How do we find happiness in the midst of an imperfect world? We all ask this question and go through these struggles in some way and at some point in our lives.

My own quest led me to look for fulfillment in external things. In school, I spent countless hours making people laugh in class instead of paying attention, hoping to be noticed. I went from one girlfriend to the next trying to find fulfillment. I intensely sought meaning in sports. I was obsessed with exercising, and I worried that people didn't like me.

I found things that satisfied me in the moment, but when the temporary fulfillment subsided, I didn't know what to do or where to turn. I was afraid of silence, and I was afraid of solitude (now I crave both), so I filled my life with busyness, noise, living moment to moment.

Momentary happiness is an epidemic in our culture, and I was addicted to it. We are often afraid to carve out space in our lives for deep introspection and contemplation, so we continually try to fill the void with something else. Some of the things we do are harmless, and some are toxic. Either way, satisfying our longings with momentary spurts of happiness gives us superficial consolation and not authentic fulfillment. Things that are external make us feel good, and we can even be applauded for some of them. Accolades and achievement can drive our identity. Then who we are is all about what we do and what we accomplish. Yet how long can those feelings sustain us? I can't be team captain, honor-roll student, and class clown my whole life, can I? I can't keep trying to win the same titles as an adult that I won as a teen and think they will make me happy.

It's like a jet burning out of fuel—it's a joyride, and the landing can be quick and rough. I've had that feeling—the one where I couldn't go on any longer. When I was a young man, my life looked great from the outside. I was doing well in school. I was successful in sports and had friends and girl-friends. Yet on the inside, my need was huge. I was starving.

Fr. Alfred Delp, who is famous for leading the Catholic resistance to Nazism in Germany, states, "The created being must cry out to some power beyond itself in order to acquire its share of strength; when we realize and acknowledge that our natural powers on their own are inadequate we have taken the first step towards salvation."[1]

Not long after attempting to drive my truck off the road, I came to a place where I cried out and took a step to discover God. I began to discover his life, mercy, love, and joy; but I was still fragile.

My adult years lay ahead. Although I began to find truth, I still lacked the deep roots to move forward on solid footing. I started to seek less toxic things, to set positive goals, and I pretended my life was great. I was "sailing around the world" while still searching for fulfillment.

The "less toxic" things are the things that are more difficult to recognize as problems in our life. For example, I was a per-fectionist, which meant I accomplished things and did things well—but I really had a fear of failure, and my outward suc-cess hid it. This perfectionism allowed me to do good things and accomplish goals I set; yet even this became an obstacle for me.

I enjoyed college and continued my search for happiness there. Like many young adults, I stayed busy and distracted enough to avoid reality. My faith and my search somehow conflicted. I was lost and found at the same time.

We all eventually land on the question of happiness, because we all want the answer, the key, the formula. We crave happiness more than anything. It's not that we *deserve* happiness, because that signifies that we must earn it and somehow be worthy of it.

The reality is we don't deserve, can't earn, and don't merit happiness because we are *already created* for it. Because we are created for it, we crave happiness, and we will continue to starve until we find it.

REFLECTION QUESTIONS

1. In what ways do you find yourself "starving"?
2. What do you use to satisfy your cravings?
3. What's your goal in life?
4. At this moment, what do you see as your purpose in life? How are you fulfilled (or unfulfilled)?
5. What is it that you seek? What are you hoping to find?

CHAPTER 2

IT'S TIME TO SURRENDER

It was a beautiful, clear evening. I could smell the fresh-cut grass and hear the sound of fans cheering. Playing baseball in college was my dream, and I was living it!

I remember when I threw the ball from right field and watched it bounce before it reached the infield. I looked at my left arm, my throwing arm. It was dangling from the socket. A sharp pain, like a knife stabbing into my skin, ran from my neck to my numbing fingers on the left side of my body. Something was terribly wrong.

When the doctor entered the room, x-rays in hand, I could tell the news was bad. All I could think was, "You have to fix this so I can get back in the game. My future in pro baseball is at stake here." Even when he said I had three fully torn ligaments in my throwing arm, I still held out hope that my life plans would be realized.

I knew I couldn't throw a ball until it was fixed. All I wanted to hear was how long it would be before I rejoined my team. What I didn't know was that I could barely move my left arm without the ball completely falling out of the shoulder socket.

The doctor gave me two choices, both involving surgery. With the first procedure I could play baseball again, but it came with warnings. I could rehab and have a chance to play, but I would probably need several additional operations down the road if I played long-term. This option also had serious implications for the future. Within ten years, I would no longer be able to throw anything, and I would face years of chronic pain as I aged.

Most people wouldn't even consider this option, but as a college athlete, I saw sports as my life. I had totally invested myself in baseball and football. I had trained for this nonstop since I was a child, and my sacrifices had been monumental. When an athlete plays on that level, there is no question when it comes to risking your body in the short term in hopes of playing for one more day. I didn't want to hear the other option, but he told me anyway.

Option two was to completely overhaul my shoulder, which meant grafting and repairing the ligaments and implanting screws to hold the grafts together. With this procedure I would probably never need another surgery and would be able to throw again after a long and extensive rehab. This sounded good. I could get back in the game. I knew I could cut my rehab time to eight or nine months with the kind of dedication I was willing to devote to the process.

But there was a catch. After surgery and rehab, I would have only 80 percent mobility and range of motion in my shoulder for the rest of my life. For most people, 80 percent might be good, but to play on the college and professional level, competition is so tough that the extra 20 percent is the difference between making it and not making it. This option meant walking away from competitive sports. I had planned my entire future around playing ball. This setback would ruin my dreams.

I was at a weak point in my life—physically, spiritually, and emotionally. I didn't know what to do or which way to turn. St. Paul's words about God being strong in our weakness stared right at me (see 2 Corinthians 12:10). I began to pray and "lean into" the grace of God, seeking his will and trying to gain understanding.

It's often said that if you want to make God laugh, tell him your plans. I think God was tired of laughing at me. My plans had run their course, and for the first time, I was actually willing to consider God's plans for me.

I struggled with letting go, but I knew that there had to be something else for me. It was during this time of deep introspection that I began to see, for the first time, what it was I truly desired. All along God was preparing me for marriage, for being a dad, and for a new career path that I had never considered. I didn't have a wife yet, but God knew that for me, throwing a ball with my children—children I didn't even have yet—and coaching high school football and Little League baseball would one day mean so much more.

The decision to forget the dream of a lifetime and forfeit years of dedication and training was not simple. God never said it would be easy, but he did promise that he would be there with us.

When I left my sports career behind, it felt as if I jumped off a cliff. The only way to get air in a parachute is to jump. I had to trust that God would blow air in my parachute and catch me on my way down. He did, and he had something much better for me than I could have imagined.

Behind the scenes of my athletic endeavors, I had begun to uncover another passion. I wanted to tell others what God had done for me. I wanted to help people search themselves, find God, and embrace true happiness. I started to do this in what might seem an odd choice of places—among teenagers, most of them from broken homes and broken communities. I was just out of my teens myself, and I had no idea where this would lead. All I knew was that I needed to follow the path of fulfillment instead of contentment, so I pressed on.

More than twenty years later, I look back and remember and realize I could have taken the other option. I don't know where it would have led me, but I know that this road has taken me to authentic happiness and boundless fulfillment.

I've spoken to more than a million people, started a non-profit to help the underserved, and have mentored countless teens and adults—all by allowing God to take over my plans. Most important, I met and married the most amazing woman who helps me to experience true happiness every day. She and our five kids were never in my plans, and now I can't imagine life without them.

God's plans are far greater and better than any plans we can dream or hope for ourselves. Scripture tells us this: "For I know well the plans I have in mind for you—oracle of the LORD—plans for your welfare and not for woe, so as to give you a future of hope" (Jer 29:11). I am a witness to this every day, seeing God's plan unfold in my life.

Many times in life we stand at a crossroads, wondering which fork we should take. God's ways are not our ways: "For my thoughts are not your thoughts, nor are your ways my ways—oracle of the LORD" (Is 55:8).

There can be scary moments in our lives. How do we move forward? How do we find fulfillment? Which is the best route to take? How do we know God's plans for us? In times of adversity, doubt creeps in and grabs hold of us.

I believe that there are only two options when we come to a crossroads—there is no middle ground. We can choose the path of surrender or the path of doubt, control, and fear. For me, control is a second hat—it is comfortable and even fashionable at times. But control can have a bad look—just ask those who struggle with the control of addiction or some other compulsion. Control can also have a "sexy" look and make us feel as if we have it all together.

I finally figured out that people who "have it all together" are only pretending they are in control. None of us are really in control, and we are foolish to think otherwise. I'm not saying that taking action, making changes, setting goals, and making good decisions doesn't matter. We should take control over the parts of our lives that cause us to form good habits and let go of bad ones.

Control is an outward appearance with an inward reality that eventually takes shape somewhere in our life. I believe that at the root of control is fear, and when we come to acknowledge and embrace our fear instead of running from it or pretending it's not there, we can arrive at a place of surrender.

Why is surrender a good thing? Surrender gives God the ability to work, move, and intervene in our life. Surrender gets "us" out of the way. My baseball injury is just one example of the many times I've had to surrender, allowing God to take over.

Cardinal Joseph Ratzinger (who went on to become Pope Benedict XVI) defined conversion: "'Conversion' (metanoia) means . . . to come out of self-sufficiency to discover and accept our indigence."[1] Authentic freedom comes when we totally surrender!

Now, I want to introduce you to one of the bravest women in history: St. Joan of Arc. Joan was a fifteenth-century French maiden who fought for truth during a time of great adversity.

At the age of nineteen, she was burned at the stake for standing up, speaking out, and defending truth.

Joan grew up as a peasant's daughter in medieval France. Her mother instilled in her a great faith, which Joan as a young woman passionately claimed as her own. Joan had a deep devotion to God, talking to him as though they were best friends. Motivated by her faith, Joan took action at fourteen, defending against the attacks of pagans upon her homeland, the king, and the Church. This was unheard of for women at the time, but Joan had a purpose. She was driven by God to do something greater than she could do on her own.

Joan was captured during a revolt against the Burgundians. She spent over a year in prison, refusing to agree to false accusations against her. On May 30, 1431, Joan was put to death, burned alive for her steadfast faith. In one creative adaptation of Joan's life, she states, "One life is all we have and we live it as we believe in living it. But to sacrifice what you are and to live without belief, that is a fate more terrible than dying."[2]

Someone who has never experienced true happiness can't visualize it. I remember taking a group of students on a trip from Arizona to the coast of California. Arizona, as a landlocked state, doesn't have a coast. Many of the students I was with had never seen the ocean in person. I grew up in Louisiana and had never known anyone who had not experienced the beauty of the open waters. On the trip over I tried to explain what the ocean looked like; but for those who had never experienced it, it was only in their imagination or what they'd seen in pictures and videos.

I'll never forget when our bus pulled up on the Pacific coast. The first-timers took off out of the bus—without permission—and ran, fully clothed, into the ocean. What they had imagined in their minds was nothing compared to the experience of seeing the ocean and jumping into it for the first time.

Knowing authentic happiness is the same way; we somehow need to see it, run into it, and embrace it for ourselves. I know the sun exists because I see its light and feel its warmth. I know happiness is real because I've seen it and tasted it. Do you know true happiness?

During our talk on the plane, my co-traveler Walter said, "You say God is your source of joy. Don't God and happiness only exist if you think they do?"

"If I told you gravity didn't exist and was convinced that this was true and then decided to jump out of this airplane, would I still fall?" I asked.

"Yes, you would fall and die."

"So gravity exists no matter what we think, right?" I asked.

"Yes, absolutely!" Walter agreed.

We can't see gravity, but we can see its results. It's a similar situation with happiness. Gravity and happiness are real, no matter how much or little we have experienced them or what we think about them. They are what we call absolute truths. We can't pick and choose what is true and what isn't, because what is true already exists. Things are real or not real. Truth is truth, no matter what we think! That's what I mean by "absolute truth."

Happiness was set in motion, like gravity, from the very beginning of creation.

The best place to begin our search for happiness is on the foundation of truth and reality.

"If gravity is true and real, is it possible that truth exists?" I asked Walter.

"Yes," he agreed.

"So if truth exists, is it possible God exists, too?"

"Yes."

"OK. If it's possible that God exists, is it possible that he is the creator of truth?"

"Yes, it's possible."

Truth is just as real as the sun or gravity. We can't always fully explain these things, but we can certainly point to evidence that proves they are true.

When I see in others or experience for myself authentic happiness, I know it's real and true. St. Thomas Aquinas, drawing on St. Augustine before him, explains our created desire for peace: "Everyone desiring anything desires peace, insofar as one who desires anything, desires to attain, with tranquillity and without hindrance, to that which one desires: and this is what is meant by peace, which Augustine defines as the 'tranquility of order.'"[3] This "tranquility of order" that Augustine talks about is a created desire that every human being has. You and Walter have it, I have it. We desire peace and happiness.

It isn't easy to think "beyond oneself"—beyond what is obvious, explainable, and touchable. Many will argue that faith is a blind decision. Others will argue that it's silly to have faith and that we should only go by what is certain and evident.

We don't live by faith alone but rather stand in the middle of faith and understanding (reason). Reason helps us to think logically, to research extensively, and to explain that which is often difficult to understand. You could say we have a "faith seeking understanding"[4] of things.

Faith and reason complement each other, and neither stands alone.

"Faith and reason are like two wings on which the human spirit rises to the contemplation of truth; and God has placed in the human heart a desire to know the truth—in a word, to know Him—so that, by knowing and loving God, men and women may also come to the fullness of truth about them-selves,"[5] states St. John Paul II.

St. John Paul II was a philosopher; he understood that the human heart is designed to know truth. He understood that the human mind is a seeker of truth, knowledge, and under-standing. And he understood that it is with faith and reason that the human spirit contemplates truth and ultimately finds the fullness of truth, "by knowing and loving God."

Why is faith something to run from rather than something to run toward with an open mind? Faith is not blind accep-tance or a decision made from nothing. Faith is an informed decision that takes in all of reality based on truth.

Don't we all use faith, even if we claim we don't "have faith"? Do any of us have certainty about our jobs or future? Do we have certainty that we are safe in our homes or driving to work? Do we have evidence of how long we will live? The answer to these questions is no, we don't know many things in life with certainty, yet we live with faith in life, even when we don't know it—because faith is a gift of grace that is part of who we are as humans.

In faith, the human intellect and will cooperate with divine grace: "Believing is an act of the intellect, assenting to the di-vine truth, by command of the will, moved by God through grace" (*CCC*, 155). God gives us the grace to have faith. And God chooses not to hide from us. He reveals himself to us in many ways, increasing our faith. By grace and through divine revelation, we come to a deeper faith and understanding.

God gives us the faith to stay, to believe, to know, even when we are not 100 percent certain. When we commit to mar-riage, faith is the belief that the person who's walking down the aisle is the same person whom we are there for in the first place, even if it hasn't been revealed. More generally, faith is taking in all of reality and allowing ourselves to make the right decision in each moment by grace, through revelation and reason.

Faith is jumping into the ocean, even though it may be the first time we see it, and surrendering to the larger reality that is God. Faith is permitting ourselves to experience the beauty, majesty, and truth that go beyond the surface and into the depths of our hearts. Certainly faith can be scary, but life is scary anyway, with or without faith. However, with faith, there is a deep knowing that *all will be well*. We have support, we will not be alone, we will survive—even in times of difficulty.

The emptiest people put faith in themselves or things rather than God. The happiest people I've met are those who have faith, not in themselves, others, or things—but in the reality of God.

"What about things that can't fully be explained?" Walter asked, referring to what is known as mystery. Many of us, myself included, are afraid of mystery—what reason can't explain. As humans, we are afraid of the unknown. I can't see the future, and at times it frightens me. The future is, and always will be, a mystery. But not being able to fully explain or know something shouldn't keep me from living life to its fullest.

Imagine running away from your wedding because of fear and lack of certainty. Is what lies behind the veil worth the risk?

I remember standing at the front of the church many years ago and asking myself as Gretchen walked down the aisle, "Can I do this? Is this real? How do I know it will work out?" All I could do in that moment was trust that the mystery of the unknown would lead me to a greater sense of happiness. At the time, I was as prepared for the moment as I could be, but I certainly wasn't fully equipped for everything that was in front of me. Who is? We face the unknown and the inexplicable every day. We live most of our lives not fully knowing what's around the corner.

Why should we live in fear rather than surrender?

"A mystery is not something you can't know anything about, but is something that you can't know everything about."[6] God is mystery, and it's in his mystery that we get lost in the reality of faith, hope, love, and joy; and our fears subside. Can we explain everything about the mystery of God? If we could, then would God even be God?

As a human, I'm limited in my capacity to fully comprehend, explain, and define God . . . what I can't fully explain, in my limited human mind, is the mystery of God. Yet what I do know, what God continues to reveal to me, is more than enough to satisfy me until my life ends.

My life took a turn after my sports career ended—a turn I could never have predicted or imagined. This turn brought me to a place of deep surrender to God. I didn't know what was next for me, but I knew I had to trust and let go. I had to trust that the happiness I desired and the life I was created to live were not in the rearview mirror but ahead of me.

Like Joan of Arc, I want to die knowing true happiness.

REFLECTION QUESTIONS

1. Are you at a weak point in your life? Spiritually? Physically? Emotionally?
2. How do you struggle with letting go?
3. Are you ready to trust God's plans for you? Why or why not?
4. What area of your life is the most difficult to surrender and entrust to God?
5. Do you have faith? Where do you get it?

CHAPTER 3

RETHINK HAPPINESS

I remember "falling in love" for the first time. I was in the third grade, she lived in my neighborhood, and I spent many afternoons and Saturdays riding my bike in front of her house hoping she'd notice me. Occasionally, the kids in the neighborhood would all play together—when she was there, it was great. She would flirt with me. I was smitten. And I was certain the feeling was mutual.

On one particular day, a good friend and I walked in front of my crush's house, and she was on her front porch. With him by my side, I took up the courage to walk over, and we all began to talk. I can't remember the conversation, but to me it was a big deal. I was glowing. I'd been brave enough to make my move, and I just knew it would pay off. I'd fallen for her, and hard.

As we left her house and walked down the street, I heard the words I'd been waiting to hear. She had moved to the edge of her porch, and when we were just out of sight of her house she yelled, "I love you!"

I couldn't believe it—this was it! As her words reached my ears, I stopped. My heart was pounding, and I turned back toward her house. I cupped my hands around my mouth so the sound would project far and loud, and at the top of my lungs I screamed, "I love you, too!"

I had finally expressed my love for her, proudly, for the whole street to hear. And she responded, "No, not you!"

At first I was confused. Then I understood. She was expressing her feelings for my good friend standing next to me. Apparently they had a thing, and I was totally unaware of it.

How did I not see it? How could something that seemed so real in my head and heart be completely fake? The whole thing was a scam, a counterfeit. I had invested my heart and time in something that wasn't there. Maybe I was clueless, or maybe I was just in denial. Whatever the reason, my feelings for her had blinded me to the truth, but now my eyes were open to the reality that not everything is as it seems. It was my first memorable encounter with the idea of something being counterfeit.

A counterfeit is an imitation or a fake replica of a real product—it is the illusion that something is real or authentic. There are many counterfeit products out there, and often it is difficult to determine the difference between the real product and the fake one. Counterfeit money is an easy example. Fake money has been around since the introduction of currency. Thieves have produced it in hopes of becoming wealthy. Good counterfeit bills are hard to recognize—so much so that the FBI has trained agents solely devoted to catching both novice and professional counterfeiters.

The FBI training process begins with developing the ability to identify real money. The agents learn to recognize what is authentic by studying valid bills closely to become intensely familiar with the real thing. Once the agents are fully aware of the appearance and feel of real bills, they are tested with counterfeits. Blindfolded and not blindfolded, the agents are given both fake and real bills to sift through and separate. Over time, trained agents can spot a counterfeit bill by sight or touch with great accuracy. Imagine applying this skill to your own search for happiness—the ability to see immediately the difference between temporary pleasure and lasting joy.

I spent the first twenty years of my life seeking things that didn't satisfy me—things that were counterfeit. I searched for a feeling, a moment, a success, a comfort, an accomplishment, an affirmation. I had moments of happiness seeking these things, but my search seemed endless and unsatisfactory. I remember thinking, *Is there a pinnacle to happiness? Can I truly be fulfilled?* I also remember some of my greatest successes leaving me empty. How could this be? I was achieving goals, yet these accomplishments didn't translate to anything substantial or long-lasting.

I could pretend to be happy around others, but deep inside I was empty and unsatisfied. My outward success and persona only masked what was going on internally—a deep longing to be fulfilled and happy.

Richard Challoner, a bishop in England in the 1700s, refers to experiences like mine as "painted bubbles": "Honors, riches, and worldly pleasures are all but painted bubbles, which look at a distance as if they are something, but have nothing of real substance in them, and instead of a solid contented joy, bring nothing with them but a trifling satisfaction for a moment followed with cares, uneasiness, apprehensions, and remorse."[1] These words ring true even in our world today. Our human desire, our created heart, longs for more. We long to be fulfilled by more than pleasures.

Bishop Challoner's words remind me of what is arguably St. Augustine's most famous statement. As a bishop in Hippo (in modern-day Algeria) in the late fourth century, he wrote this eloquent passage in his *Confessions*: "Thou hast made us for thyself, O Lord, and our heart is restless until it finds its rest in Thee."[2]

These two bishops from vastly different cultures and times are essentially stating the same thing. They both tell us that we are seekers who desperately desire happiness, and in our search we will be disappointed in anything short of finding God.

Many years ago, I gave a talk to a group of young people at a conference. I thought it went well—I had presented the material the organization requested. When I opened the floor for questions, I braced myself for potentially argumentative confrontations, knowing that I was dealing with an audience of teenagers. In these moments I'm usually prepared, or pretend I am, for anything that may come my way. I receive a range of questions: How old are you? Is God real? When is the world going to end? Who's your favorite superhero? This time, however, I wasn't so much surprised by the question itself but by the way in which it was asked. A young man whom I will call Wayne stood up in the back of the room and asked me to explain whether I thought people should wait until they are married to be sexually active. (This question comes up often, but Wayne had a bitterness in his voice I couldn't interpret.)

Because this is a serious question, I took time to explain the practical, spiritual, and emotional reasons why saving sex for marriage is best for our well-being and happiness. I explained that God created sex to be good and sacred—a powerful sacramental union between husband and wife.

Wayne's girlfriend sat next to him with her head down in embarrassment as he responded. "I hear everything you say, but I don't agree with you!"

"OK, you don't have to agree with me, but it doesn't mean that what I'm saying isn't true," I replied.

"Well, whether it's true or not, I'm going to do whatever I want to do and whatever feels good to me," he said.

I've heard that response from many people. I've even said a version of that myself, something like, "I'm going to do things my way." I'm sure you can relate to some version of doing things "your way," too.

When Jesus says that he is the truth, he is not making a suggestion—Jesus is making a statement, letting us all know that he is the "way and the truth and the life" (Jn 14:6). Jesus' words do not depend on majority vote; they exist as true no matter what we think. Truth and reality exist together, to keep our minds and hearts set on what is good, authentic, and beautiful. Jesus—"the way." He leads us to "the truth and the life" we long for. In him we find our way. In him we find truth. In him we find life.

That's not such an easy concept to swallow, however. We all tend to want to do whatever we choose, sometimes ignoring truth and reality. The word for this tendency is *concupiscence*. According to the *Catechism of the Catholic Church*, "'concupiscence' can refer to any intense form of human desire. Christian theology has given it a particular meaning: the movement of the sensitive appetite contrary to the operation of the human reason. The apostle St. Paul identifies concupiscence with the rebellion of the 'flesh' against the 'spirit'" (*CCC*, 2515). It is the battle between good and evil, truth and counterfeit.

Wayne (the kid from my presentation) went on to say in front of the crowd, "And I can fix or protect myself from any complications that may arise from my decisions to do what I want." The crowd began to laugh. I let the young people settle down and responded calmly and lovingly:

> You can do whatever you want, whenever you want, and how you want; it's called free will. However, Wayne, there is nothing you can do to fix or protect yourself from the very thing that you are seeking deep down inside— to be loved, to be satisfied, and to be happy. What you are looking for can only be found in something greater than momentary feelings, emotions, and actions.

Wayne was immersed in counterfeit happiness and couldn't see past the illusions of what was real and not real.

After the session concluded, Wayne and his girlfriend remained sitting alone. He stopped me and asked if I would be willing to talk with them. I agreed and sat down beside them. Wayne said, "I'm really just trying to justify my actions, but the reality is neither of us is happy. We love each other, but we really aren't fulfilled." His girlfriend nodded in agreement as tears ran down her cheeks.

Sadly, they were both lost on the journey, letting emotions determine their decisions. They were fooled by counterfeit love and no longer knew what was real or substantial. Underneath their confusion, however, was a deep longing for true fulfillment. They had become lost and disconnected from reality in their encounter with the counterfeit.

I parted by reminding them God loves them, even in their mess. And I encouraged them to allow God to change their hearts and help them commit to a relationship of chastity and authentic love. Years later they married, and now have a beautiful family.

As I reflect on Wayne's situation, I'm reminded of just how essential it is for us to understand that as humans, we are more than our emotions. We don't operate on mere instinct but with intellect and reason, too. Just imagine if you and I were simply emotional beings, and we lived only by what satisfied our flesh. We would be less than human, for the soul gives life to the body and meaning to our lives.

The *Catechism of the Catholic Church* tells us: "The unity of soul and body is so profound that one has to consider the soul to be the 'form' of the body: i.e., it is because of its spiritual soul that the body made of matter becomes a living, human body; spirit and matter, in man, are not two natures united, but rather their union forms a single nature" (*CCC*, 365).

Basically, what we do with our body uniquely affects the soul because the two are unified. We are body, soul, will, intellect, and emotion—thankfully, we aren't made simply of feelings. If this were the case, our decision making would fail us when our emotions do. And we all know that our emotions can easily get the best of us.

Just imagine how our lives would be if we acted on every moment of anger, lust, greed, envy, comparison, hurt, or apathy. In my own life experience and in dialogue with others, I've noticed that much of our trouble and regret springs from moments of making decisions based on how we feel. This is tantamount to the FBI agent using only his sense of touch to detect counterfeit bills. He is handicapping his own ability to know the truth! The same happens when we rely only on our emotions to make judgments.

When we begin to understand our whole self, created in the image of God, we start to make decisions recognizing the true over the counterfeit. This is the way to genuine freedom and happiness.

Fortunately, we are already created with the full capacity to choose good and to know authentic beauty, to avoid the traps that lead to regret, and to strive for interior peace.

"God willed that man should be 'left in the hand of his own counsel,' so that he might of his own accord seek his Creator and freely attain his full and blessed perfection by cleaving to him" (*CCC*, 1730). The *Catechism* goes on to say, "The more one does what is good, the freer one becomes. There is no true freedom except in the service of what is good and just" (*CCC*, 1733).

So how do we get to that place of freedom?

During my college baseball days, I went through a major hitting slump. My initial reaction was to try harder, work longer, practice more. So I worked out more, practiced longer, and mentally challenged myself to push through the slump. These were all good things to do, and often they worked. Yet I remember a coach telling me, "You're trying too hard. It's like you're holding on to the game so tight that you're afraid to let it go; you are 'white-knuckling' it." He was right: I was so focused on the slump that the slump consumed me. I had lost focus on the game—the fun and the routine of playing. I was determined to pull myself out of the slump. But holding on too tight only made me lose control even more.

Ask any golfer if holding a golf club tightly is a good thing. He will quickly tell you no. A loose grip keeps the golfer relaxed and fluid in his swing. When he holds on too tight, he doesn't allow his body to naturally take over, releasing his athletic instincts. Ultimately, the tension and tightness in his body force the swing off track. A difference of centimeters in the swing of a golf club, tennis racket, or baseball bat can mean the difference between reaching par, acing a shot, or hitting a home run.

The same thing happens in life. When we hold on too tight, we fail to let God do his work. Call it control. Call it fear. Call it lack of faith. When we are lost, we grab tightly to whatever we think will save us. I have found that the more I grasp for control, the less control I actually have, leading me to feel trapped and unhappy.

So how is it that we can make sound decisions if we don't have control? It's God's grace, of course. By his grace, we choose good, and by choosing good, more grace follows. God's grace is much stronger than our nature because grace is the gift of God himself, and by his grace we can do anything.

Grace is God's presence in our life. Grace gives us the ability to take a step forward, and when we do, grace pushes us even further in the direction of good.

Paul explained it to the Romans this way: "But if by grace, it is no longer because of works; otherwise grace would no longer be grace" (Rom 11:6). And the *Catechism* reminds us that it is "by grace that we are saved and again it is by grace that our works can bear fruit for eternal life" (*CCC*, 1697).

God, who is grace, is the only one who can pull us out of any slump we are in and get us back on track. He instills in us a new heart, a heart that seeks goodness, beauty, and truth. The enemy, however, wants us to keep our old heart—a heart that beats off rhythm and sways back and forth between good and evil. He wants us to be stuck in a "hitting slump" and pushes us toward a life of self-reliance and "white-knuckling." The evil one knows that if we live this way, we will live exhausted, defeated, and unhappy.

The last thing my coach told me was, "The game finds you, you don't find the game." I was trying to find the game. My efforts, though good, couldn't force the game to get easier. I had to let go!

This is true in our lives. We can't force things to go our way. We may be able to succeed and accomplish things, but along the way we will eventually exhaust our efforts and crash.

In the same way, we can't find God or his grace. God finds us and gives us his grace freely because he loves us! *We* can make life happen on our own terms, but we will tire out. *God* can make life happen for us, moving us to a place of true freedom. He holds the whole of creation in his hands and holds us in his hands as well. Our exhaustion in life should not lead us to more self-reliant ways of living but should lead us into the arms of God, who offers us a much different picture and a much greater purpose for happiness.

How do you surrender to God and allow his grace to pervade your life? How does the process of "rethinking" begin and lead us to deeper happiness? These questions were ones that

I wrestled with for years, and I continue to learn more about these issues every day.

Then-cardinal Ratzinger offers us some help in answering these questions:

> The Greek word for converting means: to rethink—to question one's own and common way of living; to allow God to enter into the criteria of one's life; . . . begin to see one's life through the eyes of God; thereby looking for the good, even if uncomfortable; not aiming at the judgment of the majority, of men, but on the justice of God. . . . Unconverted life is self-justification (I am not worse than the others); conversion is humility in entrusting oneself to the love of the Other [God].[3]

These words bring to light just how far self-reliance can take us from the love of God, who requires us to recognize our dependence on him in all things. Self-reliance is the part of us that seeks to live life on our own terms and by our own strength. I'm a sucker for this! I believe in hard work, in preparation and pushing myself to be better. These are good qualities to have. Yet the self-reliance that I'm speaking of is one that leaves God, his presence, and his grace out of our lives. When I try to live and act without my love for God as the primary motivation for my actions, I am using self-reliance. When this happens, I end up exhausted, stressed, and confused.

I know many people who are very successful living this way. But outward success doesn't mean that they have inner peace. Take Walter, the CEO, or many others I have encountered who are successful by worldly standards yet still looking for authentic happiness. How can one have it all and yet have very little?

Through a number of conversations, the CEO who bought all the cars saw his need to surrender and ask God to enter into his life and his heart. His conversion began right there, as he started to see his life through a different lens, to turn his mind, heart, and soul to God. Conversion can start with a moment when we completely turn to God and to a new way of living. But conversion is a process. It involves rethinking the way we understand happiness and surrendering to God every day. This allows him to lead us. When we surrender and trust in God's way, we begin a journey toward true freedom.

It is God who stands on the front porch and yells to me and you: "I love you! Yes, you!"

In the next chapter, we will unpack the ways in which we can respond to him.

REFLECTION QUESTIONS

1. What in your life is counterfeit? Are you surrounded by counterfeit happiness?
2. What are some of the things in your life you insist on doing your way, not God's way?
3. In what ways do you have concupiscence—an intense form of human desire that goes against what Gods wants for you?
4. What or whom do you base your truth and happiness on?
5. What do you need most in your life?

CHAPTER 4

KNOW YOUR DESTINATION

About ten years ago, I found myself sitting in the home of a well-known NFL football player. I knew him from watching him play on TV. I was a fan, but I wasn't there to get his autograph or take a selfie with him (though I wanted to). I was there to meet with him about some issues he was having in his life. As we talked through his problems, it was apparent that his newfound fame wasn't bringing him the satisfaction he thought it would. His life looked different on the outside than mine did, but inside his heart, he was struggling with some of the very same issues you and I have.

His situation was complex, and his fame only complicated things. He confessed that he thought once he signed a big contract and reached the pinnacle of his sports career, everything would be great. He found out quickly that arriving at fame, money, and success didn't change the problems in his personal life. His heart was longing for deeper satisfaction.

I've noticed in my own life that happiness has often been connected to moments, goals, and accomplishments. And when the satisfaction that came from an accomplishment faded, so did my happiness. I often thought, *When I reach such-and-such a goal, then I'll be happy*. Like my pro athlete friend, I believed that arriving at a certain destination would give me what I was seeking.

This is what I call destination happiness. And I have exhausted myself in pursuit of it.

Destination happiness is a mentality that says, "When I arrive at a certain point in life I will be happy." For example, we might say to ourselves, "When I am married," "When I find a different job," "When I earn more money," "When I become a parent," "When others recognize my talents," "When I buy a new car," or "When I get a promotion." The list goes on. It's not that the things on our list or the destinations we seek are necessarily bad and won't bring us some satisfaction. These achievements can be good things and can bring joy to our lives; but they don't bring us lasting fulfillment in themselves.

Destination happiness often begins at a young age and is based on external accomplishments. Parents affirm kids for a great game played or good grades; later, bosses promote employees for making a sale. Affirmation for an achievement brings joy, but like all things, the accomplishment of the moment wears off. The destination is no longer paradise.

I know personally the exhilaration of reaching a goal and the satisfaction of achievement, but I can honestly say that those feelings never gave me the lasting peace I desired. In my years of ministry, I have met with many people who struggle with the same thing. I see firsthand how easy it is to get trapped in the mind-set of destination happiness. It is common to lose sight of what authentic happiness is.

When we seek happiness by reaching a destination, we set our sights on the mirage that is ahead of us and not on the reality that exists, which is God. The destination we were created for is God alone. And finding our meaning in who God made us to be is the only paradise that will satisfy our longing.

Success is a popular word in our culture. There are countless books written about success and how to achieve it. We are attracted to the idea of success because as humans we desire to reach our full potential. Success is a good thing. Our work has meaning!

Yet success in itself is not a destination that will make us happy. People who *redefine* success and place it in proper perspective have a much greater chance of finding lasting joy than those who make success their final destination for happiness.

There are plenty of CEOs, doctors, teachers, stay-at-home parents, retail workers, ministers, oilfield workers, farmers, and others who do their work well, but job success isn't their destination. What I mean is that the frantic search to make money or gain success isn't the reason they work hard. Interestingly, some of these people make a lot of money and some make very little, yet they are equally happy.

I eventually came to a place, a state of being, where I rooted my life in authentic happiness. I finally started to understand what Jesus means when he says, "Blessed are they who hunger and thirst for righteousness, for they will be satisfied" (Mt 5:6). I was and still am hungry and thirsty. But now I understand that a life devoted to Jesus is the only path to eternal happiness.

The football player I met with told me he longed for more, just as you and I do. Listening to someone who had so much recognize the voids in his life helped me realize that we are all tempted to land at destinations we think will satisfy us.

Happiness is our destination. Everyone longs for it. And everyone is meant for it. But it isn't found where we often land. *Happiness is found in landing at a place of surrender to God.* When we say, "I give you my life" or "I let go and give you control," our surrender ushers in God's grace. His grace sustains us through the times when we struggle to find our purpose and our meaning.

Surrender first requires that we identify our priorities in life. What matters most to you? For me, the things that matter have evolved over time as I have gradually zoomed in on what is essential to my life. My quest for happiness took a detour filled with distractions and influences that didn't fulfill me. I tried to run away from home as a kid wanting to escape the pain of our family. I fell into bad relationships with girls, thinking they would make me feel better about myself. I built a reputation of having it all together so that even my best friends didn't know the misery inside my heart. I put my identity in what I did—sports, work, and even ministry.

We often connect our happiness with the amount of influence we have or the recognition we receive from others. We long to be known, to be noticed, to be someone special. Don't we? This is not necessarily a bad thing since we are created to be in relationship with God and with others. Relationships are important for our well-being. Yet for some reason we aren't content with just being who we are and being loved by those closest to us. We want more!

We watch those who are famous and wish we had their lives. We look at those who seem popular and want to be like them. We see those who have the stage and we want to be there with them. The advent of the Internet and social media has given all of us a powerful platform for recognition. Anyone can be noticed now! For many, the goal is to be "liked," "retweeted," and "followed." The Internet also allows us to look into the window of the lives of others we don't even know and compare ourselves to them. We become trapped in a state of constant comparison.

I once met with a person who struggled with a deep-rooted addiction to pornography. Fueling his addiction was his tendency to compare himself with others, which fed his deep insecurity. He would log on to social media, look at the successes and highlights in other people's lives, and conclude that he didn't measure up. This feeling of inadequacy prompted his slow descent into depression, which triggered harmful habits such as overeating, self-harm, and viewing pornography. Over time, as he began to accept himself as good regardless of how he compared to others, his compulsive and addictive behavior decreased.

So what's the answer? Will being liked by others make me happy? What is it that is really important to me? I have found that those who are truly happy share three traits:

1. *They know that their identity comes from something greater than themselves.* They have landed at a place in their lives where they understand that their true identity comes from the one who created them, God. This realization crafts a deep sense of surrender and humility in their hearts. There is a peace that surpasses all other things when we realize we are created and loved by God.

2. *They understand that they are a child of God.* And because we are the sons and daughters of God, we are never alone. He is always with us and created us specifically for this

father-child relationship with him. Those who have this sense of identity in Christ don't worry about "being known" because they are already known.

3. *They surround themselves with people who aid them in their relationship with God and love for truth.* This aspect of happiness requires the avoidance of those who bring lies and confusion with them, and an effort to surround ourselves with those who remind us of our true identity. Such people help us know our true destination. We are better because of them, and we grow by being around them.

Surrounding myself with people who help me spiritually has been one of the hardest and most important efforts I have made in my journey toward happiness. We all need people in our lives who help us become better. Any successful marriage consists of two people who make each other better by consistently speaking truth into each other's lives. Having friends, family, and a spouse who remind me of who I am has radically changed my life, and I've seen these relationships transform the lives of others.

We aren't meant to "journey at life" alone; we are meant to journey in authentic relationship with others who help us along the path of happiness. If we acknowledge God as our Creator and understand our true identity as his sons and daughters, and if we have people who speak truth in our lives, we begin to experience the authentic happiness we long for.

So what's most important to you? Take some time to reflect on this question. I know that for me, when God is first in my life, I am settled into who I am as his son and I'm less tempted to try to be someone else.

Have you ever thought to yourself, *If I had more money, I'd be happier*? Money gets our attention. Without money, we struggle to eat and have shelter. With it, we have power. Surely we have all seen both the good and the bad that money can bring into our lives. But can money make us happier? Interestingly, research demonstrates that after we meet our basic needs, there isn't much difference in happiness between those with a lot of money and those with very little. In other words, money doesn't affect our level of happiness once our basic needs are met. Other things matter: relationships, faith, outlook on life, pain, lack of forgiveness, hurts, brokenness, and so forth.

In my work as a speaker and mentor, I have spent significant time with people on both ends of the financial spectrum. In my own life, I've seen myself get distracted by seeking more comfort, more success, and more of what money can provide. At one point, I thought being wealthy would actually make me happy. I've also flirted with the other side of the same coin—thinking that if I lived more simply, I'd find true happiness. I'd fallen for landing at these destinations.

Thankfully, in this period of confusion, I turned to scripture for answers. I began to ask questions and seek God. Scripture states, "For the love of money is the root of all evils" (1 Tm 6:10). This verse provides a pretty strong statement, yet we can't learn everything that God wants to teach us about money from one sentence. If we consider the big picture, there is much more at play here. Paul, writing to the disciple Timothy, is hinting at something. It's not really about the *money*— it's about being *attached* to money. It's about being sidetracked by the lure of money and the things of the world. Being attached to money is what steals our joy and peace. In fact, being attached to anything outside of God steals our joy and peace. We can't be free to live and to love when we are attached to something other than God. Attachment takes away our freedom to choose and our freedom to respond.

We've all heard the saying, "If you love something, let it go." Why? Because if we hold too tight to something or someone, we can't fully love, we can't fully see, and we can't fully give. In the same letter to Timothy, Paul speaks about detachment: "For we brought nothing into the world, just as we shall not be able to take anything out of it" (1 Tm 6:7). Detachment is knowing that nothing really belongs to us. Everything belongs to God. We are created to live in freedom, detached from earthly possessions and at peace with what we have been given. We are simply passersby on this planet, waiting and longing for the day we will live forever with God, our true destination. Those who experience detachment find authentic joy in their life.

Generosity is key to living a life of detachment. Giving isn't *monetized*. Giving is a way of life, a posture of being. Many people say they will give when they have more, but having more doesn't always translate into generosity. I've seen people with very little share with others what little they have, and I've also seen those with plenty give plenty. Both are inspiring. The one with plenty isn't more generous than the one with less; they both give what they have, because they want to.

Scripture highlights both ends of this spectrum of generosity. The Gospel of Mark tells the story of a poor widow who has only two small coins, which she offers to the temple (see Mark 12:42–44). Jesus takes note of her generosity and points out her action to his disciples, not because he is impressed by the amount but because she freely gave what little she had. Her act touches his heart. This image helps us understand real generosity.

On the other end of the spectrum is Zacchaeus in the Gospel of Luke (19:2–8). Zacchaeus is a wealthy tax collector.

History tells us that tax collectors in those days were unpopular and greedy individuals. Zacchaeus has these traits, yet a significant encounter with Jesus initiates his conversion. You could say he began to *rethink* his ways. He first seeks forgiveness for his mistakes, then decides to give away "half" of his possessions. We don't know the monetary worth of half of his possessions, but it was obviously a generous gift. And I'm certain he was happier for it.

So who gave more, the widow or Zacchaeus? Neither, because giving isn't about the amount; it's about the heart. Both gave generously from what God had given them.

Relationships play a vital role in our lives. We are meant to love and to be loved. This is good. Nevertheless, we can often find ourselves hurt, broken, or unsatisfied by human relationships. Our longing to be in relationship, to be loved, to be wanted or needed, becomes entwined with our deep desire to be satisfied. And we begin to stuff our emptiness with *people*.

This is what I call the "people-sized hole"—a destination that is tricky to explain but is certainly worth exploring. Ask yourself: Can a person or a group of people fulfill me or make me happy? The answer is both yes *and* no. That's because relationships are vital to our happiness, but they aren't the crux of it.

How often has someone disappointed you? How often have human relationships (even good ones) fallen short of your expectations? We have all been on both ends of disappointment—being a disappointment *to* others and being disappointed *by* others. It's part of being human. Some of us have experienced more hurt than others, but we have all encountered the fragility of humanity. It's eye-opening when we realize that the people we love the most and who love us the most are actually, like us, imperfect.

Imperfection is not a reason to give up on people. Rather, it should prompt us to acknowledge that a person can't be a means for satisfying our deepest longings.

In marriage, we see the imperfections in the person we love. All our issues come to the forefront. In even the best marriages, two imperfect people live together in an imperfect world. Often people think, *When I marry this person, he or she will change*, or *After we're married, this person will make me happy*, or *This person will meet all my needs and desires*. Reality eventually sets in when we recognize that our spouse sometimes falls short of our expectations. They are as imperfect as we are. This doesn't diminish the wonderful aspects of marriage or the person we marry; it's simply the reality of the relationship.

My wife, Gretchen, would agree to this in our own marriage. At times, especially early on, disillusionment set in as our expectations were left unmet. It was a surprise to both Gretchen and me to realize that our strong love for each other was imperfect. We fell, and still fall, short of "completing" the other. And even with the best of intentions, we sometimes fall short of each other's expectations. I must admit, on my best day, I can't complete anyone. I am not created for that. I can certainly help—I can love, and I can give. But I can't complete someone, and neither can you. Completion is left up to someone much greater. Completion is God's job. In his letter to the Corinthians, Paul reminds us that God is "all in all" (1 Cor 15:28). He alone fulfills what is lacking in our hearts.

I have seen many people land at this destination—expecting someone to fill their void. Whether it is a spouse, a parent, a friend, or a boyfriend or girlfriend, we find ourselves wanting more from that person than they can give. I remember as a young adult feeling happy when my friends were around; when everyone left, I'd lie in bed alone and feel empty. My "happiness" faded once I was by myself. I remember being confused by this: How could the people I liked the most not fulfill me? How could a dating relationship not satisfy me? I also recall being surprised that loneliness didn't leave once I got married. How could I be in love yet lonely? Married couples face loneliness frequently. Often they try to fill the void with something or someone else. I eventually came to a place where I was willing to ask the question, "What or who can fulfill me?"

Let me tell you two true stories, about two loving married couples, that are similar but with different outcomes. Both marriages were hit with tragedy: the wives were diagnosed with terminal illness. The illnesses were different, neither had an immediate timeline, and both couples faced a long road ahead. Both men tried hard to see their wives through this tough time. The difficulty and the weight of things wore on them. The reality that their spouse could no longer love them back the way they were accustomed to set in. This would be difficult for anyone.

One of the men began to fill this void by partying with friends while his wife lay at home sick. We all need friends, but he sought from his friends fulfillment that only God can provide—and he eventually filled the void left by his sick wife with another woman. He chose, while married, to live another life, landing at a destination he thought would make him happy. By the time his wife lay dying, the family, who felt enormous grief over the loss of a loving wife and mother, was destroyed by the husband's actions. The other man sought comfort for his pain and grief in good friends who invited him to fill his void with something more substantial. His search led him to a point where he was faced with an emptiness so deep that only God could carry him across the abyss of pain and grief. He and his family found happiness in the process, joy in the suffering. And the love he showed his wife until her death brought joy, hope, and peace to himself and to his children.

Both men experienced great pain, yet one of them found happiness in the process. Why?

You may have heard that we all have a "God-shaped hole" in our hearts—a hole that only God can fill. This is a good metaphor, but I think it falls short.

Rather than a hole in our hearts, I think we each have a void—a bottomless pit that swallows up anything we attempt to fill it with. If we could peer into this void, it would be like looking out into space—farther than the eye can see and more than the mind can imagine. To call it a hole limits its size.

Also, to suggest that God *fills a hole* limits the reality of who God is. God is vast, beyond what our minds can imagine, and he is more than willing and able to fill our void. God doesn't want to plug a hole in your heart; *he wants to encompass your soul.* Using money, relationships, material things, or status to fill our void is only a quick fix. Our hearts are made for more, for God. And the real destination we are made for is knowing God and allowing him to fill our hearts. "May he draw our hearts to himself, that we may walk in his ways" (1 Kgs 8:58).

I ended my meeting with the pro athlete by praying with him and his girlfriend. I saw God move in their lives and fill their hearts with joy that day. They surrendered their life to God; and their void became God's destination.

REFLECTION QUESTIONS

1. What matters most to you?
2. What will make you happy? Is that a destination?
3. Where does your identity come from?
4. Who do you surround yourself with?
5. Do you have a people-sized hole? Who can fill it?

CHAPTER 5

KEEP IT REAL

Bungee jumping was not my idea. Four of my friends dared me, and before I knew it, I was twenty stories high looking down at a cement parking lot. I'm afraid of heights. That was over twenty years ago, and I'm still afraid of heights today. Standing on the platform of a crane, my toes inching toward the edge, my heart beating so fast I could barely breathe, I tried to pretend it wasn't real, a dream of sorts. Reality set in as they strapped the bungee round my waist and threw me off the edge. I sped to the ground and a large rubber band became my only hope for survival. This was real!

Reality exists outside of one's thoughts and emotions. The sun exists whether I believe it or not. I'm really married whether or not I feel emotionally connected to my spouse that day. I really have to pay bills. I really gain weight if I eat too much and don't exercise. I'm really getting older. I'm really tall. I'm really a man. I'm really grumpy when I'm hungry.

Reality exists no matter what our thoughts or ideas are on the subject.

Reality can be a good thing. The reality that the weather is sunny and cool puts me in a good mood. The reality that my wife is committed to me gives me joy. The reality that my breathing keeps me alive is essential. The reality that I have a loving family and good friends is fulfilling.

However, reality can also be difficult and hard to face. The sun can be so hot my skin burns. The reality that my parents divorced stinks. The reality that I wrecked my car is inconvenient. The reality that I lost a loved one hurts. You get the point.

I've noticed that people, myself included, sometimes escape into "nonreality" instead of living in the true present moment. Why? Because reality is often hard, and escaping helps ease the tension. Have you ever wanted to forget reality for a while? This is why we get lost in a movie, search the web for hours, or go fishing all day. It's also why we may leave home and not come back, fall into an addiction, quit our job, eat or sleep all day.

The trap is thinking that escaping will make us happy. We often wonder, "What's out there that I'm missing out on?" "If I only didn't have to deal with this." "If only my life were better or different." These kinds of thoughts lead us away from coping with reality.

When I was in campus ministry at the University of Louisiana at Lafayette, I met with a twenty-two-year-old student struggling with anxiety. In our conversation, he confessed he would escape for five to ten hours at a time playing video games. He said his stress led him to the virtual world, where he hoped to leave his anxiety behind. It never worked. Actually, the opposite happened. He would be more stressed after escaping into the virtual world because his to-do list only grew while he was away. His problems were still there at 3:00 a.m. when he stopped playing games.

I met a woman through my work who admitted that she would spend hours shopping online, reading blogs, and trolling on social media. Before she knew it, half her day was gone. She felt more overwhelmed and moodier afterward. Her pattern of escaping was subtle, but its effects were real nonetheless.

I'm not suggesting that video games and browsing online are bad things. With the right intention and in moderation those activities are fine. There's nothing wrong with allowing yourself time to unwind, get away, and reenergize from the craziness of life. Rest, relaxation, vacation, exercise, reading— all are necessary for our health and sanity. A game, a weekend outdoors, or a movie can be good for the soul. Yet there is a difference between relaxing from the stress of our life and trying to escape the reality of our life.

I've seen grown men and women get lost in nonreality through the Internet and books. The lure of pornography, gaming, social media, and other online activities is dangerous to our freedom. Novels, magazines, and other printed material can also be a trap.

A friend confessed to me that his wife read a sexual fantasy novel. For a while, it "spiced up" their relationship, but soon they fell back into their old patterns. Instead of engaging in their marriage, his wife began to emotionally disconnect. The book had lured her into an image of their marriage that wasn't real and never could be.

I've seen people escape into work, hobbies, and even into their minds. People escape through relationships, partying, isolation, daydreaming, and fantasies about what could or should be. I've even seen people escape into their religion, overspiritualizing their issues and creating a "sacred" place where they don't have to deal with problems.

Many of my conversations with people today run the course of self-dislike. I often hear, "I wish I were someone else" or "I wish I had someone else's life." If we are honest, we'll admit we compare ourselves to others. I've heard it said that men compete and woman compare. The root of each is the same. I think one of the greatest tragedies is trying to be someone other than who we were created to be.

When we don't know who we are, self-dislike creeps in, and we aim to be something or someone we're not.

I can remember moments in my life when on the outside things seemed fine, but on the inside, I wanted to be someone else. Being someone else seemed better because I didn't like myself. I didn't feel this way all the time, but when these feelings came they were difficult to stop.

Is being someone else a better option? Can we end old and negative behaviors and begin new ones?

I believe we can walk in freedom from the past. We can learn new behaviors that give us better results. I know this to be true because Jesus offers us a new life. He brings healing, forgiveness, and mercy to our broken heart. We see this play out in the story of the woman caught in adultery (Jn 8:1–11). This was a grave sin and, at the time of Jesus, an act that carried a death sentence. Yet Jesus intervened. He distracted and convicted the woman's naysayers. He entered her world, bringing his mercy and forgiveness. Her encounter with Jesus brings transformation. Jesus tells her, "Go . . . [and] do not sin any more" (Jn 8:11). He challenges her to leave her old ways and embrace a new way of living. Tradition tells us that she became a follower of Christ.

I've always been competitive. I was told to reach for the stars, and I did. I set lofty goals, and I attained some of them. I love the feeling of accomplishing a goal.

I've also failed at reaching some goals. I've experienced disappointment when something didn't pan out. There have been many times in my life when failure paralyzed me, gripping me and strangling the life out of me. I'm sure you've felt disappointment or failure in your life as well. It hurts.

I once met with a forty-year-old man who told me, "I'm not always happy." I said, "Explain." He went on, "Well, I just don't always feel happy and I want to be happy all the time."

The idea of being "forever happy" is simply a myth. God created us to be happy. We can certainly experience joy, but we can also feel pain, hurt, and failure. We can feel the burden of disappointment. Jesus experienced pain and sadness. We see him weep at the tomb of his friend Lazarus (Jn 11:35). We also see Jesus sweat drops of blood in the garden of Gethsemane before being handed over to his death on the cross (Lk 22:44).

I'm still learning that true happiness isn't an emotion but rather a way of life where we belong solely to God. Authentic happiness isn't a feeling but rather a state of being. What I call "the art of living" is being with Jesus no matter the circumstance. The art of living is not escaping reality but rather living in reality with Christ even though it is difficult.

I love the passage from the book of Isaiah that speaks truth into who we are: "Thus says the LORD, who created you, Jacob, and formed you, Israel: Do not fear, for I have redeemed you; I have called you by name: you are mine" (Is 43:1).

Who we are is connected to *whose* we are. Who we are—we are God's son or daughter, created by his wonderful hands.

Whose we are—we are God's; we belong to him, and nothing can take that away.

Escaping is like deferring payment on a bill that's due; we put off dealing with our life in hope that it will correct itself. It never does. So what's the answer?

Adam and Eve lost their way and God searched for them. He brought them back into reality, back into relationship with himself. God is the greatest reality that exists for us. And it is in relationship with God that we find freedom from escaping.

We must make a conscious effort to live in the present moment with God. Our intentions can be good, but intentions go nowhere unless we make a decision to act on them.

I can intend to live in the present moment and not escape from reality, but if I don't make a decision to act, nothing changes. If I go back to my old ways of thinking, I get nowhere. When we make a choice to live in the moments of our day and to be present to the reality of these moments, we experience the life that we were created for. It is in the present moment that we find the grace of God.

God is always in the present moment. He is with us, no matter the situation, in every moment of our day, helping us write our story. When we find ourselves being pulled away, it's important to recognize the crucial things that bring us back to reality.

Gratitude has a powerful way of pulling us back to reality. When you feel yourself escaping or sinking, begin the practice of gratitude. Say or write down the things you are grateful for. Try it. I do this constantly in my life. When I feel overwhelmed by life and want to escape, gratitude brings me back to reality and gives me a sense of joy.

Another way to avoid escaping is by being honest. Name the thing or things you are struggling with. Name and claim the emotion; own it. If you are sad, lonely, stressed, hurt, or depressed, name it and give it to God. Ask the Lord to be with you in the emotion you are struggling with. God is in the moment with us at all times. Honestly facing our feelings keeps us in the reality of life.

Prayer prevents us from escaping, too. If I could sum up prayer in one phrase, it would be "having a conversation with God." Prayer is the best way to stay in the present moment and to live in the reality of our life. Scripture says, "God is really in your midst" (1 Cor 14:25). As our hearts and minds converse with God, we become aware of the reality of his presence in our lives, leading us through our day. Prayer pulls us out of our old habits and negative thoughts and into the new life that God desires for us. Prayer helps us rely on God and allow him to take control.

In prayer, God reaches in and opens our hearts. In prayer, we enter into God's world, he enters into ours, and we see our lives in a spiritual reality where everything, no matter the circumstance, will be OK. I will speak more on this later in this book.

Surrounding ourselves with the right people can also help us live in reality. When we are tempted to escape, people and community can keep us anchored. We all need people we can be ourselves with—our authentic selves. Authenticity isn't a sign of weakness but of strength. And being real around our friends allows them to enter our world, helping us to overcome what we can't overcome alone.

God's forgiveness helps us live in reality. Guilt and shame for our sins, wounds, and brokenness can cause us to hide. We need to know that God's mercy, forgiveness, and grace are available to us. There is nothing more powerful than being forgiven and being loved unconditionally. God's mercy allows us to walk in the reality of who we are as his children. Although we all have a tendency to try to escape reality, we also have a desire to be authentically happy. Our desire for happiness is ultimately fulfilled by living in the present moment, with God. God's mercy and love are always in the present moment.

God's love helps us live in reality. It's true! When we realize the unending love that God has for us, we are changed. God's love is always present to us, in every moment of every day. St. John Paul II said, "Faced with problems and disappointments, many people will try to escape from their responsibility: escape in selfishness . . . escape in indifference and cynical attitudes. But today, I propose to you the option of love, which is the opposite of escape."[1] This "option of love" is found in the One who is love, God himself. And being in relationship with God will bring us true happiness and fulfillment. Scripture says, "For God is love" (1 Jn 4:8).

One of the most important things lacking in our culture today is true mentorship, where someone teaches another the art of living. I need this. You need this. But how do we learn how to live? Who teaches us the art of living?

Before I got married, I spent time talking to older married men who I knew had good marriages. I took notes, paid attention to their advice, and looked for character traits that made them good men and husbands. Over time, I applied some of what I learned to my own marriage.

I've utilized this process of mentorship in all areas of my life, and it's been a saving grace. We grow when we learn from others in areas that make us better. We tend to model the behavior of others, so it's natural for us to imitate traits of those we admire or those we are around—the question is who.

The art of living is learning, knowing, and living the life that God created us to live. This art, the life God designed for us, can't be learned on our own. Following the example of others can be good or bad or a mixed bag of life lessons, you could say. Who can we depend on to teach us the art of living?

Recently a young man, around twenty years old, asked if he could meet with me. I wasn't sure why, but I agreed and we met at a local coffee shop to talk. I asked him if there was anything specific he needed to talk about. He pulled out a notebook and said, "I just have a lot of questions about life I need advice and guidance on." He wanted to know the art of living.

The art of living is the desire of every human heart, and it's a desire given to us by God. We are created to live life to the fullest, in freedom. We are created with the natural ability to live as God designed. But having the desire to paint and learning how to paint are two different things. Jesus teaches us the art of living by modeling for us the life we are created for.

Jesus accompanied the disciples, walking with them, teaching them how to live. The disciples followed him and paid attention to his ways. They learned the art of living from his words and his example.

As children, we modeled our parents, siblings, and other relatives. Growing up, some of us had good mentorship from others, and some of us not so good. Jesus invites us to model our lives after his. Like the woman caught in adultery, we will find happiness by leaving our old ways behind and learning a new way of living, with Christ.

The best direction we can take is to embrace the person God made us to be and to become his. When we know who we are, when we discover our true self and our true identity in God, we find our meaning and purpose for existing.

There are two roads we can travel.

The first road leads to a mediocre version of who we are meant to be. I've met many miserable people who are disenchanted with life, traveling the road of unhappiness and discontent—and I've never met anyone who, deep inside, wanted to be that way.

The second road takes us to an authentic, fulfilled version of who God made us to be. This occurs when our identity as God's son or daughter sinks in and determines our reality, every day.

Which road do you want to take?

If our identity comes from what others think of us rather than who God says we are, we define ourselves by what others have done to us, what mistakes we've made, or what we've done to others. Although these things are tangible and do impact us, they don't define us!

Who we are holds much more power than what someone says about us.

Who we are holds much more weight than our mistakes.

Who we are holds much more water than our brokenness.

Who we are is much more than even our successes.

St. John Paul II said, "*We are not the sum of our weaknesses and failures; we are the sum of the Father's love for us and our real capacity to become the image of his Son.*"[2] God, our Creator, defines who we are and gives us our true identity in his image.

We can have "self-discovery," but we can't discover our true selves without discovering who we are in the hands of the Creator. The truth of who we are in God's eyes is key to finding authentic happiness.

"Let us make human beings in our image, after our likeness. . . . God created mankind in his image; in the image of God he created them; male and female he created them" (Gn 1:26–27). We are his daughters and sons.

When our identity becomes clear, we are set free to live the authentic life God intends for us to live.

The biggest game changer in my life was discovering who I was. For a long time, I put my identity in what I did. Over time, God showed me that my true identity isn't in what I do but in who I am. I am God's son, no matter what.

Our journey in discovering God and finding true happiness begins here. You are his, and you belong to him. This is not a myth; it is truth, and it is the reality we are called to embrace and live.

God is more secure than a big rubber band posing as a bungee cord. As we live in relationship with him and grasp the reality we were created for—the reality of being his—we lose our fears and begin to trust in him.

REFLECTION QUESTIONS

1. When do you find yourself wanting to escape reality? Why?

2. What part of your life do you find difficult to keep in reality?

3. In what ways do you find prayer, recognizing God in the present moment, difficult?

4. How are you becoming who God wants you to be?

5. Where do you find your identity? Does God define who you are?

CHAPTER 6

RECOVER WHAT WAS LOST

About fifteen years ago, I was invited to speak at a large Catholic conference in Atlanta; about forty thousand people attended. Don't get the idea that I'm important. I wasn't the keynote speaker—I was just giving a talk for the youth and young adults, alongside the larger adult event. It was like being the opener for the main band at a concert.

I checked into the hotel and received a speaker's packet with the info I needed for my sessions. I made my way through the halls of a massive conference center as thousands of people checked in and wandered around waiting for the talks to begin. I was proud to be a speaker. The map in my hands led me down halls that seemed to run in circles. I was lost. Eventually I stumbled on an oasis—the speakers' hospitality room, a big arrow labeled "Speakers" pointing to it. Most of these rooms are simple, stocked with a few bottles of water, granola bars, maybe some fruit. Sometimes there is a couch to rest on and a comfortable place to work on presentations, as well as Wi-Fi.

This room was different, impressive. There were leather couches, an all-you-can-eat buffet of real food, a wide selection of drinks, even a chocolate fondue fountain. I thought to myself, *I'm in heaven.* I grabbed a plate of food and looked for an empty chair. A woman doing her job came up to me and, very politely but firmly, said, "Hey, you aren't supposed to be in here." I thought to myself, "My name tag says SPEAKER!" She looked down at my badge and said, "Oh, you're one of those youth speakers, aren't you?" I dropped my head and looked at the small piece of prime rib in my hand. "Yes, ma'am," I said. *Maybe she'd feel sorry for me and let me stay.* Nope. She said, "OK, there's a youth speaker room somewhere else." I was one of only two youth speakers at this conference.

I put my plate down and felt a hand on my shoulder. A soft but stern voice, accented, said, "He can stay!" I thought, *Yes!* The woman was surprised. I must admit I looked at her with a little smirk, then turned around to see who saved me. It was a man dressed in clerics, black suit and white collar, with a pectoral cross—worn by Catholic bishops—around his neck. He extended his hand and said, "I'm Cardinal Oscar Rodríguez." I thought, *Huh? A cardinal!* This was a big deal. I was not prepared or dressed for the occasion. I had on a pair of jeans, a T-shirt, and sneakers. I couldn't hide my shocked expression as I put out my hand and said, "Hey bro, I'm Paul." *I called a cardinal "bro"! Oops!*

He gave me a forgiving smile and said, "Sit down and have lunch with me." The cardinal and I sat down and had an amazing conversation.

I didn't know it at the time, but Oscar Rodríguez is a longtime cardinal and the archbishop of Honduras. He is known worldwide, sits in the inner circle of Church authority, and meets with the pope to help make decisions for the entire Church. Rumor has it that in the last two papal elections he was on the shortlist to be the next pope. With all his authority and importance, he is a humble man.

Cardinal Rodríguez lives in Tegucigalpa, the capital city of Honduras, a third-world country. He doesn't wake up every day with first-world problems. Unlike me, his life isn't turned upside down if he loses his cell phone charger, if the traffic is bad, or if the hot water runs out. His life and inconveniences are different. He ministers to the poor, both physically and spiritually. And because of this, he sees the world differently.

The cardinal seemed content and joyful. His happiness spoke to me. My own happiness is often sparked by having access to abundance—such as prime rib in a speakers' hospitality room. His happiness is sparked by something deeper. He was happy simply sitting down with me, the marginalized in the room, talking about life.

We live in a world of marginalized people. In fact, all of us, in some way, have been on the fringes of life at times. God invites us in. Just as the cardinal invited me, Jesus invites us to dine with him.

St. Paul speaks of the attitude I saw in Cardinal Rodríguez: "I know indeed how to live in humble circumstances; I know also how to live with abundance. In every circumstance and in all things I have learned the secret of being well fed and of going hungry, of living in abundance and being in need. I have the strength for everything through him who empowers me" (Phil 4:12–13). Like St. Paul, Cardinal Rodríguez owes his happiness to a strength inside himself, powered by Jesus. He's simple, detached, and happy.

Simplicity is freedom from deceit and unnecessary complexity, the absence of luxury and pretentiousness. Simplicity has to do with ridding ourselves of that which isn't necessary. Simplicity can be about giving things away and being generous with what we have, or about simplifying our calendar and working less.

The simplicity that Jesus calls us to runs deep. To understand true happiness is to grasp what it means to be simple and to live detached, free from worries and things that steal our joy.

Simplicity of heart means having Christ at our center.

Happiness begins and ends with God—understanding who he is and his vision for our lives. Although God can seem complex, and God is *big*, that doesn't mean we can't know him. We aren't created just *to know about* God. We are created *to know* him.

We can start to understand who God is by getting to know his many character traits. He loves. He creates. He protects. He pursues. He provides. He thinks. He responds. He is simple. And he is near.

God might seem distant at times because the world convinces us that he's far away—but he's not. I've looked out at the stars and wondered where God is and if he's real. I've thought, *How can he be so far away?* I talk with many people who long to know God, who live good lives, but still feel as though God is distant.

Pope Benedict XVI said, "God is not a faraway 'ultimate cause,' God is not the 'great architect' of deism, who created the machine of the world and is no longer part of it—on the contrary: God is the most present and decisive reality in each and every act of my life, in each and every moment of history."[1]

Throughout the Old Testament scriptures, we get a clear view of God as a passionate Creator and lover, always pursuing his children, no matter how far we run. We see a God who would do *anything* to prove his love for us.

I'm a dad. My wife is a mother. Although we are imperfect parents, we'd do anything to prove to our children we love them. Rather than buying them the newest gadget, we want to sacrifice and work for their well-being, to prove we will love them no matter what they do. Most parents I know feel this way.

"No one has greater love than this, to lay down one's life for one's friends" (Jn 15:13). This verse from the Gospel of John explains God's total, unconditional love for us. His love goes beyond our human understanding because God's love is perfect, unfailing, complete. The *Catechism* expresses it this way: "God's love for Israel is compared to a father's love for his son. His love for his people is stronger than a mother's for her children. God loves his people more than a bridegroom his beloved; his love will be victorious over even the worst infidelities and will extend to his most precious gift" (*CCC*, 219).

God is a much more loving parent than I am. He's God. I'm human. On my greatest days as a parent, friend, or child, I fall short of the absolute unconditional love that God bestows on us. We can give and receive love in admirable ways. We can sacrifice and serve with a pure heart. But God *is* love (1 Jn 4:8). And the most perfect form of all love comes from him; it *is* him.

The book of Romans offers us another key dimension of God's character: "But God proves his love for us" (Rom 5:8). How does God *prove* his love?

To prove means to establish the truth or genuineness, to demonstrate validity or authenticity. God is a *prover*! He will do whatever it takes to establish the truth, to demonstrate his validity, to show us and to convince us that he loves us.

In one of the most beloved verses of scripture, John says, "For God so loved the world that he gave his only Son, so that everyone who believes in him might not perish but might have eternal life" (Jn 3:16). God proves everything by giving everything. Giving himself. Giving his son.

Authentic happiness comes from seeing ourselves through the lens of God's love for us. Seeing ourselves the way our loving God sees us.

Grasping God's love means understanding the extent God went to in order to prove his love. He sent his son, Jesus, who gave himself totally and lovingly for us. Christ came to help us rethink our lives, move our hearts, and change our minds, and to teach us a new way of living. A way of happiness. God went the distance to show his love for us by sending his son, Jesus.

God's plan to enter into society was unconventional, to say the least. I imagine God at the drawing board trying to figure out how to enter the world. I can see the looks on the faces of those gathered around the boardroom table with him—a few bigwig saints, some angels, and some Old Testament prophets. I imagine God explaining his plan for Jesus to enter the world through the womb of a young virgin and can see the incredulous looks on the faces of those at the table. They probably thought, *He's crazy*, or *Too many things can go wrong; too many variables*. That's my imagination, me as a human trying to figure out how God could do something so miraculous. Outrageous even. But God's ways are not our ways.

The prophet Isaiah says, "For my thoughts are not your thoughts, nor are your ways my ways—oracle of the LORD. For as the heavens are higher than the earth, so are my ways higher than your ways, my thoughts higher than your thoughts" (Is 55:8–9).

God didn't need a strategic planning team or a consulting firm to come in and give him advice. He didn't need an analytics specialist to give him the odds of the mission's success. Nope. God knew all along his plan would work. To us it seems impractical, risky, crazy. But God doesn't think like we do. He doesn't want our input; *he wants our hearts.* And he will go the distance to get them.

Imagine all the things that had to go as planned: Mary, a young teenager, agrees to her role after an announcement from an angel. She's engaged to Joseph and now she's pregnant, but they've had no relations! Joseph is confused and I'm sure angry, too. He plans to leave her quietly, to avoid bringing her shame. Mary has no husband and nowhere to go. Imagine. But God doesn't worry. His ways are good.

God sends an angel to speak truth to Joseph, in a dream. Joseph is the second Christian, after Mary. Joseph's heart is changed by this encounter, and he decides to stay the course with Mary and Jesus, never leaving their side.

In the midst of God's unfolding plan, there is a census. Everyone has to journey to their place of birth. Joseph is from Bethlehem, which literally means "house of bread." (Interesting that Jesus, the Bread of Life, is born in the city whose name means "bread.") Joseph and Mary travel to Bethlehem, where they have no place to stay, and no plan.

Mary gives birth in a cave. In simplicity, Jesus enters the world and is laid in a humble manger. How can God allow such injustice? Where's the limelight and the attention? Unlike me, God doesn't need a speakers' hospitality suite. His plans are far greater.

Under the influence of Satan, King Herod orders the murder of male children two years and under, to get rid of the competition—a special person, possibly a messiah. Herod orders a child holocaust, an evil slaughter of innocent lives.

Yet God stays the course. His plan must happen. God must prove his love. You and I need a Savior.

God sends an angel to Joseph a second time, now telling him to flee to a foreign land: Egypt. The family must cross borders into another country and live as refugees until it's safe to return. How would they know? There were no news channels or cell phones to keep them up to date. All they had was faith; and there is certainly no app for that. Yet in the middle of the night, a frightened teenage girl with her son in her arms and her husband at her side flee to North Africa and remain there until the death of Herod.

They live in Egypt for a few years—interesting, considering that's where generations of Israelites spent their lives enslaved. God sent Jesus back to the land of slavery. Jesus was a new sign of freedom and was there reclaiming the land. Authentic, true freedom had come.

And this is only the beginning. God began his mission on earth in the most adverse circumstances, yet he still managed to overcome darkness and conquer death. All in order to prove his love—to win our hearts.

One of the ironic aspects of my meeting with the cardinal was that I had already planned a trip to Honduras with the ministry I was running: Adore Ministries.[2] We were partnering with Catholic Relief Services to help serve the poor. During our conversation, I told Cardinal Rodríguez that I would be in his country in six months. He said to me, "When you come to my country, look me up, and we will meet again." I told him I would, but, honestly, I thought he would forget about me.

Six months later, a few of our members met in Tegucigalpa with the director and his team, who are from the area, to begin our week's work. I told the director that the cardinal wanted to meet with me while I was there. I didn't have the cardinal's number or access to a phone. I'm not at all fluent in Spanish. The director told me he had been trying to meet with the cardinal for over a year and couldn't make it happen because of the cardinal's busy schedule. I reiterated that the cardinal wanted to meet with me. The director scoffed at me and reluctantly had someone call the cardinal's office. To his surprise, the cardinal was in town and wanted to meet with us. That day!

On the way to our meeting, the members of our team each prepared one question to ask the cardinal. Riding in the back of an old pickup truck, I wondered if the cardinal would even remember me.

We met in the cardinal's modest living quarters for about an hour. We all introduced ourselves, and he remembered me! We took turns asking our one question. He was very present, sincere, and humble. I was last to ask a question.

"Cardinal," I asked, "how can we help, even more, to serve the poor of your country?" Good question, right? Especially since we were there to help the poor and raise awareness of their needs. The poverty in Honduras is great. As with other underdeveloped countries, the need for food, clothing, water, and education is critical. The work of serving the poor is mon-umental, and we must all chip away at it, both domestically and globally.

The cardinal looked at me, then scanned the room to catch everyone's attention. "It's not the poor in my country who need the most help; it's the wealthy," he said. *Gulp!*

If you know anything about Central America, you know that the gap between rich and poor people is huge. There isn't much of a middle class. A person can be riding a donkey to work on a dirt road and right next to him is someone driving a Mercedes. You can stay at a five-star hotel, and a mile away is a village of very sick people with dirty drinking water. The distance between the rich and the poor is *massive*. The problem is noticeable and frustrating.

Cardinal Rodríguez explained. "The poor in my country know that they need God. They wake up every day in need of food, water, and clothes. But many of the wealthy in my country wake up with everything they need and don't think they need God." *Whoa!*

That got me thinking: *Who are we without God?* And how sad that we often (myself included) think we don't need God! And yet while visiting the poor villages in Honduras, I noticed a certain mood. Happiness. People in every village were happy to have what little God had given them. I watched as a village of three hundred people rejoiced and celebrated when clean water came flowing from a new well. It was like manna from heaven. When was the last time you thanked God for a simple thing like water, or food, clothes, a car, or a job?

I'm poor. I may have clean drinking water and plenty of food, but I'm no different inside than those who are materially poor. I'm also rich. I may not have an abundance of wealth, but I have an abundance of blessings. I'm also spiritually rich and have been freely given God's grace. And I'm spiritually poor, having lived many days ignoring God.

I'm blessed and broken.

Jesus came into the world in poor, humble circumstances to meet us where we are. Jesus knows what it is like to be rich, to be poor, to suffer, and to die. He understands what it's like to need and to want. God becoming man allows God to be in solidarity with us. God becomes poor and lowly so he can live with us—in our poverty, our need, our brokenness.

As Cardinal Rodríguez said, the greatest poverty in the world is not lack of money; it's life without knowing God. The greatest poverty is to be spiritually broke: without God and without purpose.

The cycle of spiritual poverty can be stopped. And there is only one solution: Jesus. This is why Jesus came. This is why God's plan matters. This is why the Incarnation matters. God had to prove that we matter to him. St. Gregory of Nyssa reminds us: "Sick, our nature demanded to be healed; fallen, to be raised up; dead, to rise again. We had lost the possession of the good; it was necessary for it to be given back to us" (quoted in *CCC*, 457). God knew that we needed to find our way back to reality. He reached down to earth and became man. He lived a life we couldn't live and died a death we deserved, so we could once again live the life we were created for.

Earlier I mentioned part of a verse from St. Paul to the Romans. Here is the complete verse: "But God proves his love for us in that while we were still sinners Christ died for us" (Rom 5:8). God proves his love by sacrificing his life so that we can enjoy ours, both now and in eternity.

God's love moves our minds and hearts to respond. It moves us to *rethink* how we are living and how we want to live.

Conversion, rethinking, is both a moment and a process. There was a moment when God's truth motivated me to make changes, to turn from what I was doing and begin a new way of living. I needed to leave behind a life of sin. God's grace pushed me to walk away from "old ways" of living and begin to learn a new way of living.

It didn't happen overnight. The process of conversion continues. And God, who was consistent and patient with the

Israelites wandering through the desert for forty years, is consistent and patient with me. He offers you the same.

God meets us where we are. He proves it over and over again. You may be far away from God, or you may be near. In his letter to the Ephesians, St. Paul says, "He came and preached peace to you who were far off and peace to those who were near, for through him we both have access in one Spirit to the Father" (Eph 2:17–18).

It doesn't matter where you are in relation to God. He wants to recover what was lost, our hearts.

REFLECTION QUESTIONS

1. How is your life complicated or cluttered? In what ways do you struggle with simplicity?
2. Have you seen God prove his love for you in some way in your life? How do you need God to prove his love for you in your life right now?
3. How does God's plan for sending Jesus change you?
4. Do you consider yourself spiritually poor? Do you find that you need God in your life? Explain.
5. How can you invite God into your desires, needs, and wants?

CHAPTER 7

RECOGNIZE AUTHENTIC BEAUTY

It was winter, and I was sitting on the top of a mountain in Lake Tahoe, Nevada, staring at the most beautiful scenery I'd ever seen.

My cousin's dad, my uncle, gave us his credit card and told us to go on a trip for winter break. He said, "Go anywhere you'd like." We looked at each other and thought, *Did he just say go anywhere?*

This wasn't normal, but my uncle must have had a good year and was feeling generous. We were college kids, torn between getting jobs over the break and going on a free trip. Decision made, we took the American Express Platinum and booked a ski trip to Tahoe—two small-town Louisiana boys from the bayous, headed to the great Rocky Mountains.

From the moment we arrived, we were both captivated by the beauty of the mountains and the snow. It was majestic. This was a first-time experience for us at nineteen years old. And it was obvious we were newbies because we were the only two people having a snowball fight at the airport. We didn't care; we were engulfed in the new experience.

The morning after we arrived, we took to the slopes. We skipped ski lessons (big mistake) and made our way to the top of the mountain. Nothing could surpass the ride up the ski lift to our destination. Sitting for the first time on the summit of a mountain, thousands of feet up, was incredible. Honestly, it was spiritual. My breath caught in my throat. My heart was filled, and my soul felt alive. It's a moment I will never forget—or tire thinking of.

My friend Lance takes a group of kids from Louisiana to the Rocky Mountains on a retreat adventure every summer. The trip is called Ten Thousand Feet. He's convinced, just as I am, that if you take someone away from the craziness of everyday life and place them at ten thousand feet, their hearts and souls will be moved. And he's right. The teenagers and adults who attend the weeklong camping retreat have life-changing experiences, as I did twenty years ago.

Beauty has a way of capturing us, moving us, and transforming us. No one has to tell us something is beautiful because when we see it, we recognize it. A sunset. A full moon. A mountaintop. An ocean view. A cornfield. A painting. A movie. A song. We are made to see and know what is beautiful. Seeing something majestic for the first time is life altering, but seeing that same beautiful thing over and over doesn't degrade or lessen the beauty. It remains amazing.

Beauty has a way of lifting our souls and igniting our hearts. When we see true beauty, we recognize it immediately. It stops us in our tracks. It turns our heads. Beauty opens our eyes, and we are attracted to what is good. We become lost, captured.

Years ago, I visited Milan, Assisi, Rome, and Vatican City. It was an amazing journey. One of my highlights was the Sistine

Chapel in Vatican City. If you were to ask me what images I remember from the Sistine Chapel, I'd tell you that, without pictures, I can't remember many specifics. I don't remember the details, but I do remember the experience from more than fifteen years ago vividly. I experienced life-altering beauty.

The beauty of Michelangelo's paintings in the Sistine Chapel moved me. I was captured by it. I literally lost track of time and sat for hours staring at his depiction of creation, Noah and the Flood, and the Last Judgment. God's story was real, alive, and beautiful.

It was like falling in love and not knowing how it happened. Real beauty moves us to fall in love—to stay in love.

I had never seen mountains before my trip to Lake Tahoe. Not once. Only pictures in a magazine. Before visiting the Sistine Chapel, I had never seen Michelangelo's artwork. Only pictures in a book. Yet as soon as I saw both, I recognized true beauty.

True beauty has a way of separating itself from that which is not beautiful. And the more we are surrounded by authentic beauty, the more we gravitate to that which is good and turn away from that which is not. Just like with a cup of coffee: once you've tasted the good stuff, it's hard to go back.

Yet in the midst of exhaustion or intense emotions triggered by life's challenges, we might think something is good and authentic when it's really fake.

Work with homeless people is rewarding, but it's also difficult and sad. Not only are they in pitiful shape, but they smell, too. Joe, a homeless man I befriended, told me he'd gotten used to the smell—to the point where he didn't notice it anymore. For me, the smell is always bad. Sure, I get over it, but I never get used to it.

In many ways, Joe is no different from me. I may shower, wear clean clothes, and live in a clean house, but there are areas of my life where I've gotten accustomed to the smell. There are habits and patterns I ignore.

I remember a moment in my marriage when my wife "smelled" something on me that I didn't notice. I was used to it, but she refused to keep smelling it. The tension built.

It was Christmastime, but I was not in the holiday spirit—a pattern for me. For years, I experienced depression during holidays. I would withdraw. Sad memories would rule my mind and heart. Joy around the holidays was foreign to me. Now that I was married with kids, this attitude negatively affected the people I loved most. I was not aware that this had become an issue. My wife, lovingly but firmly, helped me recognize the pattern. It stunk. *I* stunk. She was right.

Unaware that there was a better way, I'd simply gotten accustomed to the "smell." I needed to change, to become clean. I asked God for the grace of healing and of understanding a new way to live. Jesus moved in my heart and began to heal me of my wounds. I prayed a simple prayer: "Jesus, come into my past and present and heal me. Bring your presence into the areas of hurt, pain, and lack of joy. I trust in you." Over time, very simply and gently, he restored the beauty within me. Now, years later, I experience the holidays with a sense of joy, in a new and awesome way. I even hum a Christmas carol or two!

We don't have to continue in the way we've always lived, to act or feel the way we've always acted or felt. *We aren't made to live in the dirty muck of our lives.*

We aren't created to smell.

We are created to see ourselves the way God does. We are created to recognize true, authentic beauty, and to live in that freedom.

Remember Walter, the guy on the plane who had sailed around the world? Walter had seen the beauty of the world. He had traveled to every continent and had experienced beauty I will never see; yet he had not seen the beauty of our Creator, nor the beauty in which he was created.

Walter was searching for answers. Deep answers. He wanted to know how I found truth and happiness in my life. He was searching for more than the beauty of the coast of Madagascar, South Africa, Japan, or Hawaii.

The *Catechism* reminds us, "The desire for God is written in the human heart, because man is created by God and for God; and *God never ceases to draw man to himself.* Only in God will he find the truth and happiness he never stops searching for" (*CCC*, 27, emphasis added).

God had been chasing Walter his whole life—Walter just didn't know it. God is chasing you and me as well!

Walter and I talked extensively about God during that flight. Walter had an epiphany of sorts right before we landed. He realized through our conversation that in all his travels and all his searching, God was searching for him. The moment he realized this is one I'll never forget: We were sitting at ten thousand feet, and suddenly he saw things from a different perspective. He saw authentic beauty in God and in himself, and his heart was changed.

The book of Genesis tells us that God recognized the good in what he had created (Gn 1:12). Man and woman were created good. We're still good. Yet sin enters the world. Beauty becomes tainted. We see imperfections in ourselves and in others. Like Adam and Eve, we grab hold of things that keep us hidden from freedom. We sin. We fall short. We smell.

It's like someone pours mud over the mountains. The beauty is still there, but it's hidden. Through sin, mankind no longer sees beauty. Our distance from God makes things blurry.

We read in Genesis, chapter 3, that after Adam and Eve fell for the enemy's ploy, they ran and hid in the garden (see Genesis 3:8). Makes sense to me. My reaction to my sin—when I mess up, when I disobey—is to hide. I want to disappear until it all goes away. I feel shame. I feel guilt. I feel unworthy. This is exactly how Adam and Eve felt. They understood immediately their wrongdoing. Even though they had been tricked, they knew they had disobeyed God. They felt the disappointment of their mistake and took off running into the trees.

Genesis tells us what happened after they sinned: "Then the eyes of both of them were opened, and they knew that they were naked; so they sewed fig leaves together" (Gn 3:7). Adam and Eve saw their imperfections. They thought, *God will never take us back.* They thought they could live apart from God. They thought they didn't deserve to live in Eden. Shame runs deep.

"The LORD God then called to the man and asked him: 'Where are you?'" (Gn 3:9). God didn't reject them. He didn't neglect them. He didn't even scold them. *God searched* for Adam and Eve.

I understand this feeling. A few years ago, my wife and I took our four kids to a large amusement park. We prepped them for what to expect. We explained the heavy crowds and the possibility of getting separated. Sure enough, my son, who was about five years old, got lost. It was only for five minutes, but I panicked. My heart raced. I ran through the amusement park retracing every step we had taken. I shouted his name. I must have looked like a madman. I didn't care; all I knew was that I had to find my son. And I would have searched forever.

I can only assume that if you multiply that moment by a thousand, it would describe the scene when God searched for Adam and Eve.

In 1989, Mother Teresa (now St. Teresa of Calcutta) visited Phoenix, Arizona. Most people just called her "Mother." She was a simple and humble servant of God. Believers and unbelievers alike were drawn to her simplicity and the humble work of her religious community, the Missionaries of Charity. Still today, years after her death, the sisters continue to serve the poorest of the poor in whatever city they reside.

Mother Teresa became known throughout the world and, in 1979, received the Nobel Peace Prize for her work in overcoming poverty and distress among those most in need. Interesting how a person who was so modest and unassuming could be so well regarded around the globe.

We live in a world of drama, attention, and fame. Many people search for fulfillment in celebrity, wealth, and acclaim. With the advent of the Internet, we are influenced by pop culture twenty-four hours a day. According to recent studies, most young people dream of living the life this culture glorifies: "Eighty-one percent of 18- to 25-year-olds surveyed in a Pew Research Center poll . . . said getting rich is their generation's most important or second-most-important life goal; 51% said the same about being famous."[1]

We all long to be noticed and cared for; but being rich and famous won't solve this human need. Only God can fulfill us. He alone can satisfy us. This is what attracted the world to Mother Teresa. She was joyful, fulfilled, and neither rich nor famous.

Mother Teresa didn't like the limelight. She stayed hidden on the streets of India caring for those dying, without food, medicine, or the basic human need—love. Her travels to cities around the world were rare but necessary for the sake of spreading the Good News and helping establish more missions for her religious order. What started with one sister in 1946 now consists of more than 5,000 religious in 140 countries around the world.[2]

I'm fascinated by Mother Teresa. How could a woman so small (barely five feet tall) make such an impact? How could someone so poor and simple love unconditionally? How could someone who worked in such difficult surroundings be so joyful? She would say that her work was all by the grace of God. She is often quoted as saying, "I am a little pencil in the hand of a writing God who is sending a love letter to the world."

Mother Teresa, in a sense, lived at ten thousand feet. She was in awe of God. Her unity with God drove her ability to see the world with great clarity and beauty. Yet her work was simple. Her mission was to love one person at a time. Just as God loved her, she loved others. Just as God pursued her, she pursued others. With remarkable insight, she said, "It is easy to love the people far away. It is not always easy to love those close to us. It is easier to give a cup of rice to relieve hunger than to relieve the loneliness and pain of someone unloved in our own home. Bring love into your home for this is where our love for each other must start."[3]

While Mother Teresa was in Phoenix, something happened during one particular visit to a person's home—a miracle, you could say. Word spread quickly that she would be at a certain woman's home. People packed the inside and surrounded the house. The crowds made a path for Mother Teresa to enter the house. Doors and windows were opened so those outside could look in. This image reminds me of the crowds gathering around Jesus. There is something beautiful about holiness. There is something attractive about authentic love. People gravitate toward it.

As Mother Teresa was leaving, she could barely make her way through the crowd to the minivan she was riding in. A woman reached out, grabbed her hand, and said, "Mother, please pray for my son, he's been missing." Mother Teresa looked at the woman, asked his name, and said she would pray for him.

Mother Teresa got in the van, and the driver headed off to her next engagement. They went through downtown Phoenix, a large city with a metropolitan population of more than four million.

Suddenly she asked the driver to stop and pull over. He was hesitant because the area was not safe. Still, Mother Teresa insisted that he pull the van over immediately. How do you tell Mother Teresa no? To her, downtown Phoenix was nothing compared to the slums of Calcutta.

Reluctantly, the driver stopped the van, and she got out and began to walk down the street. The organizers who were with her were appalled that she would put her safety in jeopardy. So they followed. Isn't it remarkable how we are afraid to reach beyond what is safe and comfortable?

Mother Teresa saw things differently. She trusted. And her vision was clear. Eyewitnesses say that Mother Teresa walked up to a homeless man on the street, bent down, looked at him, and called him by name. And then she said to him, "It's time to go home." It turns out that he was the son of the woman she'd met in the crowd outside the house. (*Whoa!*) She put him in the van, and they brought him home.

This story of Mother Teresa gives a glimpse into how God works. God moved in the garden in search of Adam and Eve. They were homeless. He found them and brought them back home—back into relationship with him, where true freedom and happiness are found.

God promises that he will never leave us. We may feel distant from him. We may even run away and hide, but God promises that he will search for us and be with us: "My love shall never fall away from you nor my covenant of peace be shaken, says the LORD, who has mercy on you" (Is 54:10). The letter to the Hebrews puts it succinctly: "I will never forsake you or abandon you" (Heb 13:5).

God's promises are true.

The book of Exodus tells us the story of the Israelites, working for years under bondage to the pharaoh. Their slave labor supported the bustling Egyptian economy. God promised to set the Israelites free from the Egyptians. And he did. God also promised them a "land flowing with milk and honey" (Ex 33:3). He delivered. He also promised that he would never abandon them on their journey. He stayed. He made a covenant with the people to be with them forever. And he kept it: "The LORD preceded them, in the daytime by means of a column of cloud to show them the way, and at night by means of a column of fire to give them light. Thus they could travel both day and night. Neither the column of cloud by day nor the column of fire by night ever left its place in front of the people" (Ex 13:21–22).

God always provides a sign. We see this throughout the Old Testament: The Ten Commandments. An ark. Manna from heaven. Water from a rock. A tabernacle. Angels. Prophets. Victories. A burning bush. Himself.

God's promises aren't hollow words but rather his total commitment of himself. Even with all these signs, even with God's presence, the people wandered through the desert for forty years before they reached the Promised Land. God never left them. He never gave up on them. Ever.

If you study historical maps of the Israelites' journey to the Holy Land, they basically went in circles, constantly losing sight of where they were going. Sounds a lot like me, a wan-derer. I still feel lost at times. We all wander. We all get lost. We all lose hope. And we've all hidden.

You may be lost right now or feel as though God isn't with you on your journey. You've probably felt alone or neglect-ed. You probably understand disappointment, dissatisfaction, not knowing what's next or where life is taking you. You may have experienced feeling afraid of what's ahead—but God promises to be with us. Does God really keep his word?

We live in a world where promises, contracts, and agree-ments are broken all the time. It's part of human nature. It's part of business. It's part of living in a broken world. We break promises because we can. But God thinks differently. God goes beyond a promise. God makes a covenant with us. And hopefully, we make a covenant with God.

Covenants are deep bonds between two parties to live in agreement, in relationship, and with a purpose. Covenants are forever. The Israelites made many covenants with God, sacri-ficing to demonstrate their faithfulness. They promised with their words, but they reneged. Their sacrifices were short-lived.

But God didn't give up on them. He didn't take back *his* word because *theirs* failed. His covenant is forever.

Marriage is more than a promise between two people—it's a covenant, a bond, and most importantly a sacrament be-tween a woman and a man. That bond is sealed through the power of the wedding vows, their yes to each other, forever. In the sacrament of Marriage the priest or deacon doesn't ad-minister the sacrament. The priest or deacon, like everyone else present, witnesses the couple exchange their sacramental vows. And it is God directly, through the vows made by the couple, who seals the sacramental agreement between hus-band and wife. Words have meaning. Signing our name means something, but these kinds of promises are easy to break. Our word is easy to go back on. Our world is full of people backing out of promises, even marriage.

More than words or a signature, the ultimate sign of the covenantal yes of marriage is offering oneself, one's body for the other—not just words but body, heart, and soul. A free, total, and faithful yes, sealed by the couple as they give their bodies to each other in sexual union. The words of the marital vows are finally complete in the total yes of the sacramental exchange of their bodies in sexual union, where the two become "one flesh" (Gn 2:24; Mt 19:5–6).

The giving of one's self, the sacrifice of one's body, is the true sign of forever. "This bond, which results from the free human act of the spouses and their consummation of the marriage, is a reality, henceforth irrevocable, and gives rise to a covenant guaranteed by God's fidelity" (CCC, 1640). Man and woman become one flesh, bound together forever. Marriage is a powerful covenant.

Yet even the most powerful love between man and woman doesn't compare to that of God's covenant with us.

God sent his son, born of flesh, to live among us. Jesus comes to teach us a new way of living. He teaches us how to love. He teaches us how to serve, to be humble, to forgive; how to think, act, and pray; how to mourn, to give, and to sacrifice; how to work, how to treat others, and how to communicate. Jesus teaches us joy. Yet Christ doesn't just come to teach us. If he were simply a good teacher or a prophet, his words would only be advice. Instead, they are *life-altering*.

Jesus came to set us free. Like God setting the Israelites free from slavery in Egypt, Christ comes to set us free from the slavery of sin, pain, and wounds: "For freedom Christ set us free; so stand firm and do not submit again to the yoke of slavery" (Gal 5:1).

Jesus comes to seal the covenantal agreement between God and man—the sign of God's covenant. The ultimate sign! This sign is Jesus, offering his body, flesh and blood, on the cross. Christ, the bridegroom, comes to give his total yes to you and me. As in the covenant of marriage, Christ gives himself to us, to the Church, as an offering of his eternal commitment. He gives himself freely, totally, faithfully, so that we can be free from sin and live the life we were created for. Jesus—God—gave his body, heart, and soul to prove his love for us.

But that's not the end. God restores the earth. Christ defeats death, the enemy, and is raised from the dead to new life. Christ's Death and Resurrection restore the world to God. We are set free to see beauty again—authentic beauty. We can now recognize true happiness when we see it; all things are made new again. "Behold, I make all things new" (Rv 21:5). This includes our hearts.

My friend Fr. Mark tells a story of a priest friend of his who is blind. His friend was saying morning Mass at his parish. Imagine—a priest praying Mass without the ability to see what he's doing. Yet he does it.

After Mass, as usual, he gathered his things and began to walk home. His house was in a neighborhood a short distance from the church. He walked this route multiple times a day and was familiar with every bump, step, and turn. However, on this day, as he was walking home, he heard a dog running toward him, barking. From the sound of the dog, he could tell its size and proximity. He calculated that it was a big dog, running toward him pretty fast. In the midst of the chaos, he became disoriented and no longer knew which way he was facing. He had no idea how to get home.

Understandably, he grew scared. So he prayed, "God, what should I do?"

He said he heard a soft, gentle voice in his heart telling him to stop and sit in the middle of the road. He was confused and thought, "Why would I do that, that's dumb." So he prayed again. (Have you ever done that? The "redo" prayer?) "God, I must have not heard you the first time, so let me ask you again. God, what do you want me to do?"

Again he heard, "Sit in the middle of the road." So out of desperation, and with no other options, he moved off the sidewalk and reluctantly sat in the road.

He could hear the dog getting closer. And now a car was coming toward him. He thought, "I wonder which will get to me first?" The car did, and it stopped right in front of him. A man got out of the car and called the priest by name. He was a friend from the parish. The man helped him into the car and drove him home.

The priest sat on his couch thinking about the incident. Still confused, he asked God the meaning of it all. He began to realize that the invitation to sit in the middle of the road was an invitation to step out of the shadows of being lost, hidden, afraid—*to sit in a place where he could be found.* Suddenly he understood.

This is exactly what God wants from us. He wants us to step out of the shadows of being lost, hidden, anxious, worried, afraid, and ashamed. He wants us to sit in a place where we can be found—by him. Just as he found Adam and Eve, he wants to find us. When we stop and let God rescue us, our journey begins anew. God never ceases to chase us. He never tires of looking for us. God doesn't want us to live in the shadows but in freedom. It's his gift to us—freely given.

"Let hearts that seek the Lord rejoice!" (Ps 105:3). Although man can forget, even reject God, God continues to call every person to himself, to find life and happiness. This search for God demands of us an honest intention and a sound will: "An upright heart, as well as the witness of others who teach him to seek God" (*CCC*, 30).

Our hearts are made to step out of the shadows and into the arms of God. God never ceases to come after us, to run through the amusement park like a maniac, yelling, loudly, for his missing son or daughter. He invites us to stop, come out of hiding, sit in the road, and let him find us.

Walter and I were literally at ten thousand feet when he stopped running and silently prayed. He was finally willing to step out of the shadows and allow beauty, Jesus, to find him.

REFLECTION QUESTIONS

1. When has beauty ever captured you? Moved you? Explain.
2. Have you ever been teased by counterfeit beauty? Did you think something would make you happy, but it didn't?
3. Is there a pattern in your life that you need healing from? How can Christ renew this area?
4. Do you see real beauty when you look at yourself and who God created you to be? How so?
5. When have you ever felt lost in your life, spiritually or professionally?
6. How can you stop and allow God to find you? Are you willing to let Christ move in your heart?

CHAPTER 8

SEE WITH NEW LENSES

In 2005, one of the greatest natural disasters in American history occurred as Hurricane Katrina battered the southern coast of the United States. After briefly hitting Florida and causing little damage, the hurricane regained strength in the Gulf of Mexico and made its second landfall on August 29, striking southeast Louisiana and its largest city, New Orleans. This caused major wind and flood damage to both the Louisiana and Mississippi coasts. Katrina was the costliest natural disaster in the history of our country to that point and one of the deadliest, taking the lives of more than 1,200 people. I get emotional just thinking about the many people who couldn't evacuate from the path and aftermath of the storm.

In the days following the storm, more than 80 percent of New Orleans flooded. People frantically searched for dry land, walking, riding in the back of trucks, in boats, school buses. Since most vehicles were under water, there were only a few left to transport people out of the city. I saw a car with twenty-one people in it and more than sixty people packed into the back of a newspaper truck.

To survive the rising waters, some people stole vehicles to reach safety. Good Samaritans drove their cars and boats to the edges of the water along highways to bring evacuees to dry land, to help them find a safe haven. Many people watched from afar, on television, in sorrow and disbelief. People were shocked by the physical devastation, by the poverty exposed, by the lack of organized state and national relief efforts, and by the faces of the wounded, rescued, and deceased.

For me, being on the ground and in the trenches of the aftermath was life-altering. The news media could not capture the real effects, both good and bad, of the disaster.

My family and I lived in Houma, Louisiana, about forty-five miles southwest of New Orleans. During the storm, we lost power, and the roofs of many houses, including ours, were shredded. Trees and debris covered the roads. But we were safe and dry. Cleanup began the next day. Due to the loss of power, no phones or televisions worked, leaving many of us unaware of the flooding that was starting to occur only miles away. Our city was one of the first dry towns and safe places for people from the New Orleans area to reach. Overnight, thousands of people arrived in Houma with nothing—no extra clothes, no phones, no money, many without shoes. Nothing. Tragically, many of these people also lost contact with family members in the chaos. Children were separated from parents, siblings from siblings, husbands from wives. People arrived sick, crying, in shock, hungry, and angry.

I don't have the words to describe the horror. All I know is that by God's grace, our small community was able to open up shelters in gyms, schools, and civic centers, where people could eat, sleep, and get clean. We built showers, cooked food, arranged travel, searched for family members, counseled and prayed with people.

Imagine this happening with no phone or Internet or television. In an instant, we were living in the early 1900s trying to function and take care of thousands of people. It's amazing what love accomplished as hundreds of volunteers came together to serve our brothers and sisters—a true picture of God's family—people of different races, backgrounds, and lifestyles uniting for the greater good.

Yet what we thought was going to be a week or two of relief efforts turned into a year. Most people believed they would return to their homes within a few days or weeks, but the damage was too extensive. Once the water receded, we began to shuttle people in buses to their homes to begin the process of grieving and closure.

I, along with many others, including my friend René Rhodes, could tell stories about what took place over the next year. The tragedy was vast, but God worked and moved in and through it. Miracles happened!

We built relationships with people. This is the Gospel: people loving people. We were focused on the mission of helping our brothers and sisters get back on their feet and to the new life ahead of them, no matter how long it took.

When someone asked Mother Teresa how she could take on the overwhelming task of helping so many poor people, she said, "We ourselves feel that what we are doing is just a drop in the ocean. But if the drop was not in the ocean, I think the ocean would be less because of the missing drop."[1]

It's like being on a beach, picking up one starfish at a time and throwing it back into the ocean. Mother Teresa inspired us at Adore Ministries to begin Operation Starfish, to reach one person at a time during the aftereffects of Hurricane Katrina.

In all the stories, one stands out for me. I was working in one of the main shelters, and I came to know most of the people living there. One day I went into the restroom and heard a man from a nearby stall say, "Help me!" My initial reaction was to go find someone to help him, but who? It was the two of us in the restroom. I thought maybe he was talking to himself; but again I heard, "Help!"—this time a bit louder. Reluctantly I responded, "Hey."

"Can you help me up?" Walking into a bathroom stall to grab someone is not one of the things I enjoy doing, but I had to help this guy. If not me, then who?

I walked into the stall and there, stranded on the toilet, was an elderly man, completely nude and totally helpless. Long before any relief organizations could make plans, strategize, and go through the red tape to come and help, we—normal people—did everything. There was no medical staff, not even a nurse. It was like being on a mission trip in a third-world country, but I was just a few blocks away from my own house.

I picked the man up, holding him tight so I didn't drop him. His clothes were in a pile on the ground, dirty, smelly. I'll leave the gory details out, but you can imagine the scene. I was standing in a narrow bathroom stall awkwardly holding a naked man in my arms. He was filthy, unshaven, and smelled horrible. I needed to clean him up and get him something to wear. I was too busy thinking of my next steps to even ask his name. Instead, he asked, "What's your name?"

"Paul," I said. "My name's Paul. What's your name?"

"Marvin," he said. When he said his name, what I heard even louder was, "It's me."

Huh?

I sat Marvin on the counter next to the sink; we were eye to eye, inches apart. I could see myself in the reflection of his pupils. The internal voice in my soul said again, "It's me." I thought to myself, "It's who?" Sounds strange, right? This soul voice isn't a normal occurrence for me.

Then it hit me. Staring into Marvin's eyes, I saw our differences in age, background, race—I saw the face of God. Christ was looking at me, staring into the depths of my heart. Suddenly I saw with new lenses, and I realized God's intense love for me. I understood his intense love for Marvin, too.

God does for me what I did for Marvin, except God doesn't hesitate. God picks me up when I am helpless, dirty, stinky, naked, and he carries me. He takes care of me, authentically loving me, in spite of myself. I'm his son no matter what.

God does this for you as well. God picks you up. Carries you. Takes care of you. You may not have a moment of recognition, like the one I had with Marvin, but I'm certain you can remember a time when God carried you.

In that moment with Marvin, God gently took away my old lenses and gave me new ones. These new lenses allowed me to see authentic happiness for what it truly is. Authentic happiness comes when we know our meaning as a daughter or son of God. (We touched on this in chapter 4.) "For you did not receive a spirit of slavery to fall back into fear, but you received a spirit of adoption, through which we cry, 'Abba, Father!'" (Rom 8:15). This is called divine filiation.

Divine filiation is a fancy theological term that simply means we become sons and daughters of God through Christ, the only begotten Son of God, who redeemed us. We are adopted forever into God's divine being; we are his family. We belong to God. We are *his*.

My first daughter was born with an eye condition called strabismus. It's a condition where the eyes wander, cross, and move. The doctors treated it with eye patches and then surgery.

Finally, after a few surgeries, her eyes stopped wandering and crossing. Oddly, as she aged into school, her handwriting deteriorated and her grades dropped. After talking with her, we finally figured out that she couldn't see what the teacher was doing. Sure enough, a visit to the ophthalmologist confirmed that her vision was really bad and she needed glasses. We had no idea how bad her eyesight was until the day she got her glasses.

Riding home in the car that day, she kept pointing to things asking, "What are those?" We finally realized she was pointing to trees. She was nine years old—why was she asking about trees?

"Those are trees," we said.

"Whoa, those are trees? Those used to look like blobs," she said. I don't know how long the trees looked like blobs to her, but it was long enough for her not to remember what trees really look like.

When we live outside of who God created us to be, we are spiritually blind—we see blobs. We can't recognize the beauty of things; we can't even see what they really look like. Our vision becomes distorted, and over time, life looks blurry. God longs for us to see clearly, with new lenses, and to recognize what truly makes us happy. That's why Jesus entered the world.

In the Gospel of Mark, Jesus has an encounter with a blind man in the town of Jericho. Jericho is at the north end of the Dead Sea, about fifteen miles down the mountain from Jerusalem, which was the Jewish epicenter at the time. As Jesus was leaving Jericho on his way to Jerusalem, Bartimaeus, a blind man, sat on the side of the road. Scripture tells us that there was a sizable crowd accompanying Jesus as he passed through town. Because of his condition, Bartimaeus was probably on the outskirts of town. Those plagued by ailments were treated as outcasts, unwanted in society, because the ailments were thought to be caused by sin.

Not only was Bartimaeus blind but he was also a beggar—a total misfit. He could hear the ruckus of the crowd coming. "On hearing that it was Jesus of Nazareth, he began to cry out" (Mk 10:47). He wanted to have an encounter with Jesus.

Bartimaeus was desperate to see! *He longed to know what trees looked like.* He dreamed of being treated as a normal person. He longed to see the sun, to see his family. Even deeper, he longed to know his meaning and purpose. So Bartimaeus yelled out over the crowd in hopes that Jesus would come to him.

"Jesus, son of David, have pity on me," he said (Mk 10:47). I'm sure he thought there was no hope for him, that Jesus would never hear him. The crowds tried to silence Bartimaeus, but he had nothing to lose, so he only yelled louder.

"Son of David, have pity on me" (Mk 10:48). Jesus was his only hope. He wanted to see.

Over the noise of the crowd, Jesus heard a desperate prayer in the distance. "Call him," Jesus said (Mk 10:49).

Bartimaeus was now standing face-to-face with Jesus. The crowds circled. I'm sure many people were perturbed that Jesus was taking time to chat with a blind beggar. But Jesus wasn't concerned about the crowd.

What happened next is interesting. Although it was obvious to everyone, including Jesus, that Bartimaeus was blind, Jesus asked, "What do you want me to do for you?" (Mk 10:51).

Jesus knew what Bartimaeus wanted, that Bartimaeus wanted to see. But Jesus saw past Bartimaeus's physical blindness into his heart. He desired to heal Bartimaeus's spiritual sight. He wanted conversion for Bartimaeus—he wanted Bartimaeus to see the face of God. Jesus asks the question so that Bartimaeus will begin to rethink his life and what he wants.

"Master, I want to see," Bartimaeus replied (Mk 10:51).

Jesus probed Bartimaeus's heart. Jesus wanted to heal him and set him free. "Like a physician who probes the wound before treating it, God, by his Word and by his Spirit, casts a living light on sin" (CCC, 1848).

I've longed to see, maybe not physically but certainly spiritually. This is where conversion comes in. Conversion requires us to examine our lives and our conscience—to rethink the way we live, to turn toward the new life we desire. Grace (God's presence) convicts our hearts of our sinful ways and moves us to change. God longs for our spiritual sight to be healed.

Jesus told Bartimaeus, "'Go your way; your faith has saved you.' Immediately he received his sight and followed him on the way" (Mk 10:52). Bartimaeus's eyes were opened, and the first thing he saw was the face of Christ. His life was never the same. He found meaning and purpose. His spiritual sight was restored. He received mercy, love, and forgiveness. Bartimaeus's encounter with Jesus convinced him to become a child of God and moved him to follow Christ down a new path.

Many years ago, I was directing a large youth ministry outreach in Phoenix. Each Sunday evening, four hundred to eight hundred teenagers would gather after Mass for a youth group called Life Teen. Life Teen is an international youth ministry that reaches hundreds of thousands of teens, parents, and adult leaders each year in parishes around the globe.

On one particular evening, we had a speaker, a blind woman. She shared her story and testimony of her conversion. Blind from birth, she had never seen anything in the physical world, including her husband and children. I was in the crowd with the mic for the question-and-answer session. Many of the kids asked her what life was like for a person who can't see.

Running out of time, we took one more question. A kid asked the boldest question ever: "If you had a choice between seeing your husband and kids and the beauty of creation, and being able to see spiritually, to have faith, to see Jesus and know the meaning of life, which would you choose?" *Wow!*

It felt as if the air had been taken out of the room. Silence. You could hear a pin drop. I've never been blind, and I can't imagine not being able to see my wife and kids, or drive a car, or hunt game with my dad. I've never had to wonder if blobs were trees. I'm sure our speaker longed to see her family, the sky, the beauty of creation. I'm certain there wasn't a day that she didn't wonder what something looked like or didn't think to herself how wonderful it would be to see.

As I walked over and placed the mic in front of her, without hesitation she said, "I would give anything to see the sun rise and set, the ocean. I especially long to see my husband and kids. But I would never trade that for being able to see spiritually, to see Christ and to know my purpose in him."

The room remained silent as hundreds of young people immediately were challenged to look beyond the physical, to look inward, into the depths of their hearts.

God probes our heart. He wants to heal us, to set us free, and to give us new lenses to see life with.

As the Israelites fled Egypt after generations of slavery under the pharaoh, they hurried to the Promised Land. It was the land of their ancestors and the land promised them by God.

I can only imagine the joy and anticipation they felt as they headed toward freedom. Finally, God had set them free!

The Israelites were focused on one thing, their *destination*, and getting to the Promised Land as fast as possible. But God was focused on their freedom; God knew that their journey wouldn't be easy. He even knew that many of them would want to turn around and return to the pharaoh. Slavery in Egypt had its advantages. There the Israelites had food, water, shelter. Slavery was safe. They had gotten used to the "smell" of life as slaves, and God knew that once they started their journey, they'd be tempted to turn around and go back to the familiar.

We are also tempted to turn back. But God wants more for us.

I once interviewed a man in prison. The entire time he lived in prison, he longed to be free, to live outside the prison walls, but he no longer knew how to live in the free world. Prison had become safe, so much so that he began to question whether he really wanted to get out.

I think that this is what our spiritual life begins to look like when we live apart from God. We adjust to living behind bars, and we are afraid of what our life might be like once we are freed. What would real freedom, healing, purpose, look like? We might even think about swapping authentic freedom for the comforts of a "prison cell." Spiritual apathy sets in, and we remain with the things that enslave us and hold us back from being the person God created us to be.

Our lives and our hearts aren't made to be locked up behind bars. We are made for freedom.

"For freedom Christ set us free; so stand firm and do not submit again to the yoke of slavery" (Gal 5:1). God does not want us to return to the jaws of slavery. He wants us to be free.

"Now, when Pharaoh let the people go, God did not lead them by way of the Philistines' land, though this was the nearest" (Ex 13:17). You see, the Israelites were headed one way, the quickest way, but God had other plans. Sometimes, our way, our direction, is not God's way for us. He can see farther than we can. God knows what's to come.

"For God said: if the people see that they have to fight, they might change their minds and return to Egypt" (Ex 13:17). In some translations, the scripture here says that God "thought." What did he think? God thought that the pharaoh would renege on his offer; he would come after the Israelites and force them to return to slavery. God knew they couldn't handle the pharaoh's army and would turn back.

What happens next defies human logic but reveals how God works, moves, and cares for us—how important our freedom is to God.

"Instead, God rerouted them toward the Red Sea by way of the wilderness road" (Ex 13:18). The Israelites weren't lost and stumbling their way to the banks of the Red Sea. No! God led them there. God led them to a dead-end road, and there lay a sea.

The Israelites saw the sea in front of them and the pharaoh's army behind them. They felt hopeless. They complained, as I'm sure I would have. But God was there. He was present with them. He never left their side.

"Greatly frightened, the Israelites cried out to the Lord. To Moses they said . . . 'What have you done to us, bringing us out of Egypt?'" (Ex 14:10–11). The moment of truth had come. They were ready to surrender and go back to their old way of life.

Have you ever felt like giving up? Have you ever felt like God wasn't going to come through, or there was no way out?

God is not satisfied with us going back. He wants what is best for us. He wants us to move forward, although sometimes it is difficult, to a new life with him. God rerouted the Israelites to the banks of the Red Sea because it was the best way to set them free and defeat their enemy (slavery). God rerouted them so they could rethink what they really wanted out of life. Did they really want to go back to Egypt? Or was fear just taking over? Fear of the past and fear of the future can paralyze us, preventing us from moving forward with God. But it's not up to us. God can work and will work miracles for our freedom. God wants to reroute us so he can set us free. And he will reroute us throughout our life to give us the opportunity to be set free.

As the Israelites stared at the enemy on one side and the impossibility on the other, God asked Moses to raise his hand. And the sea parted, making way for the Israelites to pass. They were free! Slavery was swallowed up in the aftermath. There was no turning back; a new life lay ahead.

The Israelites wandered through the desert for forty years before they reached the Promised Land. All the while, God rerouted them, setting them back on course and teaching them new ways of living. God is never finished with us. He desires for us to be free and to live our life looking ahead, not back at our former sinful ways.

Conversion is never arriving at a point in life and being done. Conversion is allowing God to set us free and carry us every day, by grace, to the next point in our lives. Through this journey with God, we are able to see more clearly each day.

God spares no expense to walk with us. He "rerouted" his son, Jesus, to enter the world—to bring and give us new life.

Throughout his ministry, Jesus rerouted his path to interact with and enter into the lives of individuals. In the story of Bartimaeus, Jesus stopped his journey to Jerusalem for an encounter with the blind man, and Bartimaeus's life was never the same.

On another occasion, Jesus changed his route to pass through the region of Samaria. This was not a normal route for a Jew, but Jesus knew he had to pass that way to encounter someone. Sending his disciples into town to retrieve food, he meets a woman at a well. This was not a random encounter. Jesus' intention that day was to reroute his journey so he could encounter this Samaritan woman: "He had to pass through Samaria" (Jn 4:4).

Thirsty, Jesus approached Jacob's well. It was the middle of the day, and only one woman came to the well to fetch water. It's likely that most women from the town visited the well in the cool of the morning, not in the heat of midday. They probably traveled with other women, to help one another carry the load. Yet this woman came to the well alone, in the noonday heat. She was lonely, tired, and thirsty. Her life was a spiritual desert.

Jesus didn't care that his journey took him to an isolated spot in the heat of the day. He wasn't concerned that the woman was living a life of sin and was frowned upon by the rest of her community. Jesus wanted to encounter the Samaritan woman for the same purpose he wanted to encounter Bartimaeus—to offer her new lenses to see with. He offered her "living water" (Jn 4:10). She accepted, and her life was changed. The encounter moved her to follow Jesus, to leave her old ways and take on a new life in Christ. God rerouted her that day so she could see the face of Jesus and experience true freedom and happiness. Many in her village came to believe because of her conversion.

We, too, are being rerouted. God reroutes our lives over and over so we can encounter him. When we live apart from God, we steer ourselves where we want to go, often skipping or avoiding an encounter with God. When we allow God to navigate our lives, we find happiness and freedom.

My encounter with Marvin was an encounter with Christ. God gave me new lenses to see who I really am as his son. Marvin eventually was reunited with his family and returned home.

When we encounter God in our life, we begin to see with new lenses, to see differently—and that leads us to recognize the essence of true happiness. We see our true meaning in being loved by God, by belonging to him and following him.

REFLECTION QUESTIONS

1. How does knowing you are God's son or daughter change your view of things?
2. In what area of your life do you desire to see more clearly?
3. What do you want most from God?
4. How can you allow God to transform your heart and help you to see more clearly?
5. Where do you need to be rerouted in your life? Where do you desire to be free?
6. How can you begin to allow God to navigate your life?

CHAPTER 9

TAKE THE LEAP

It was the summer before I entered high school, and my dad insisted that I find a job. I was fourteen, and like most kids my age, I didn't want to work. I had big dreams of doing nothing for the summer. However, I knew if I didn't find a job, my dad would find one for me. His options for jobs involved physical labor on a farm. The weather in Louisiana is unbearable in the summer, and his options weren't my preference. So I began to brainstorm, finally choosing the best outdoor job one could have—teaching swimming lessons.

Honestly, I just wanted to get my dad off my back about a job and get a tan before entering high school. I figured two weeks of teaching lessons would be plenty of work.

I embarked on this new endeavor with my cousin Holly. We were both newcomers to the world of swimming instructors, so we dove right in, together. The first step was to take a life-saving course in which we learned how to rescue, save, and revive a person in need. At the ripe age of fourteen, I could save a life, but I couldn't drive a car or do algebra (or any math, for that matter). The second step was to gain access to a swimming pool. My aunt and uncle, Sally and Mark (great mentors for me during a pivotal time), agreed to let us use their pool. Finally, we needed to get the word out about swimming lessons, so we put a small ad in our local newspaper.

Apparently, very few kids in our small town knew how to swim. Hundreds signed up and filled up eight weeks of summer. The good news was I had a job and was going to make money. The bad news was that I had to work all summer.

The first few weeks of lessons were easy—teaching little kids how to float, hold their breath, and have fun in the water. A nice tan and easy money! By the middle of summer, I was a pro, which was vital because this was the time older kids were scheduled to come for advanced swimming lessons. The goal for these classes was to teach different strokes and techniques.

I remember it like it was yesterday. I walked up to a girl named Amanda, who was clinging to her mother on the first day of swim class. Her mom told me that Amanda couldn't swim and was deathly afraid of the water. However, she wanted to sign up with her friends, not with the kindergarteners. The advanced swimming class was for kids who could already swim; these were mostly fifth-, sixth-, and seventh-graders. Amanda was a rising eighth-grader, meaning she was just a year younger than me, which was weird. But I agreed to help, and told her mom I'd been doing this for years (I lied) and insisted that she'd be OK. ("Fake it till you make it" was my motto.) My cousin suggested I take Amanda one-on-one for the week, and she'd take the rest of the class. I thought it would be easy. I was wrong.

It took the entire first lesson to get Amanda to put her feet in the water. By day two, I convinced her to sit on the steps, and by day three, she was willing to stand up in the shallow end of the pool. She cried for the first three days.

I've never rubbed shards of glass in my eyes, but if I had, teaching Amanda to swim was probably what that felt like. Patiently, I worked with her, determined that she would overcome her fear of the water and learn to swim. The goal of the class was to jump off the diving board on the last day, into the deep end of the pool, to show the parents what they had learned. For Amanda, I had a plan—she would jump off the diving board and I'd catch her. Together we'd swim to the side of the pool.

Friday came, and all the kids lined up to jump off the diving board. I was treading water in the deep end, watching as each kid did their thing. Parents looked on with excitement.

Amanda was last in line, and as the line shortened, I could see her anxiety rise. As she approached the diving board, all eyes were on her. She walked onto the board, curled her toes at the end, and began to cry. I promised her she'd be OK, that all she had to do was jump and I'd catch her. Our conversation seemed to go on forever. At this point, I had been treading water for a long time. I was tired. She bent down on the end of the diving board, reaching her hand toward mine as I reached up out of the water toward her hand. "Please jump," I kept repeating. "I'll catch you, I promise."

The image is still vivid in my mind. The distance between her hand and mine was literally about five or six inches. Her fear had her trapped on the edge of the diving board.

Suddenly she slipped off the edge of the diving board, landing on my head and taking us down to the drain. Lying at the bottom of the pool, I thought, "We are both doomed!" Apparently my handy life-saving skills kicked in, and I swam both of us off the bottom to the surface and laid Amanda on the edge as she coughed up water. I could barely breathe, too. Luckily we were both OK.

It's amazing how fear can paralyze us. Fear has a unique way of keeping us on the edge of experiencing the fullness of life. I've feared the past and the regret I've left behind, wondering if my mistakes would always define me. I've feared the present moment, stressed and worried about life. And I've feared the future, anxious about what lies ahead.

Fear grips us and keeps us frozen on the edge of the diving board of life. Fear keeps us from jumping into freedom.

Fear almost kept me from getting married. I can't imagine my life without my wife. But honestly, fear almost prevented me from actually taking the leap. I was trapped by the fear of "What if?" I was paralyzed by the thought of "Can I do this?" By grace, God kept nudging me to the edge of the diving board, assuring me that he'd catch me. His patience was unending as I curled my toes over the edge, fearful of the deep water. He treaded water for hours, gently encouraging me to jump, letting me know he'd catch me. And he did.

If you were to dig to the very bottom of the barrel of fear, what you would find is the desire to control your own life. When we feel out of control, we live in fear.

Remember the bungee jumping? I remember free-falling from the edge of the platform; I was afraid, naturally, because I had no control. My only hope was the bungee cord. Luckily it worked. But the cord didn't take my fear away. Fear is a natural reaction to the lack of control we have in the moment. When I landed safely, my fear dissolved. I was OK; my feet were on solid ground.

But fear can run deep. It can stay with us. When we are hurt by someone—neglected or abandoned—we have no control over the situation. The pain doesn't go away; it often buries itself and stays with us. In turn, we tell ourselves that we will have control over our lives and will not be hurt again. We unknowingly find a safe range—away from being hurt or disappointed by anything or anyone. Thus we never risk ourselves on the edge, and we miss the joy of jumping. Fear can reign in our hearts.

Replace fear with other emotions, and you and I still cling to the edge. Take regret, hurt, pain, selfishness, pride, anxiety, worry, guilt, shame, hopelessness. When these things control our hearts, they bury themselves inside us. And when we least expect it, they rear their ugly heads—telling us not to jump, to live guarded and in fear.

I'm encouraged by the words of St. John Paul II: "Do not be afraid to welcome Christ and accept his power. Help the Pope and all those who wish to serve Christ and with Christ's power to serve the human person and the whole of mankind. Do not be afraid. Open wide the doors for Christ. To his saving power open the boundaries of States, economic and political systems, the vast fields of culture, civilization and development. Do not be afraid. Christ knows 'what is in man.' He alone knows it."[1] These words mean even more in the context of Karol Jozef Wojtyla's life. He was born and raised in Poland, coming of age at the time the Nazis invaded and occupied his country. At nine years old, he tragically lost his mother, and at age twelve, his brother. Karol attended an underground seminary to hide his studies from the Communist regime in Poland, which instilled fear in the Polish people. Personal tragedy, the loss of family, and living under persecution instilled fear in Karol's heart. Yet he knew that Christ was bigger than his fear and pain. Karol let Christ reign in his heart and life, conquering the fear that had kept him on the edge, afraid to jump, as a young man. Imagine if Karol had never taken the leap to follow God's plan for his life.

It's interesting that the mere six inches between Amanda's hands and mine kept her from jumping. In her mind, six inches seemed like a mile. That's what fear does to us. Fear distorts reality. Fear takes the reality of a feeling—a natural fear, a normal emotion, a hurt, a wound, or a mistake—and turns it into something much bigger. The things that prevent us from taking the leap are also the things that keep us living in a false reality. In turn, we think the circumstances that keep us from moving forward are greater than they really are. Have you ever been fearful and made excuses? I certainly have! But imagine how your life might look if you never jumped.

If we live our lives thinking that God is smaller than our fear, then we will never be able to move forward. Happiness remains simply a concept and not a reality if we stay on the edge of the diving board. If we sit back, afraid that God can't handle what lies in our past, our present, or our future, we will live paralyzed. Stuck.

God is much bigger than our past, present, and future. God is much greater than our sins, faults, failings, and anxieties. God is larger than our brokenness, hurts, wounds, and pain. God is greater than any excuse or circumstance we can conjure up: "Great is our Lord, vast in power, with wisdom beyond measure" (Ps 147:5). God is big enough to handle anything we have.

God doesn't want us to stand on the edge of the diving board for our entire lives. He longs for us to jump, plunge into the deep end, and experience the fullness of life. We are created to jump into the arms of God. He is strong and vast enough to catch us, but we must allow his grace to move us beyond fear and into his embrace. St. John Paul II said, "People are made for happiness. Rightly, then, you thirst for happiness. *Christ has the answer* to this desire of yours. But he asks you to trust him."[2]

Jesus understands taking the leap. In Matthew 14, the disciples are in a boat miles out from the shore, traveling to the other side of the lake. In the middle of the night, waves begin to toss their boat around. They are afraid. Jesus approaches, walking on the water: "When the disciples saw him walking on the sea they were terrified." Fear set in: "'It is a ghost,' they said, and they cried out in fear" (Mt 14:26).

Honestly, if I was in a storm in a wooden boat, and I saw someone walking on water, I'd be terrified, too. But fear shouldn't guide or paralyze us, nor should it determine the course of our lives. So how do we take the leap and move forward, out of our fear?

When the disciples became fearful, Jesus said to them, "Take courage, it is I; do not be afraid" (Mt 14:27). Jesus walked into the storm and approached the disciples in their moment of need. He didn't sit back on the shore and wait for the rough winds to cease. Jesus is bigger than the storm. Much bigger.

Jesus enters our fear, too. He doesn't stand idle or at a distance. He's not afraid of our storms. He is with us in our fear, worry, anxiety, and stress. He walks with us through the storms of our lives. Just as God went looking for Adam and Eve in the garden after they sinned, so does he come looking for us. Jesus comes into our lives and into our hearts. Nothing scares Jesus, and nothing is too big for him.

The only thing that keeps Christ from moving in our lives is our "hardness of heart" (Mk 3:5). Hardness of heart is turning away from God and closing ourselves totally to his grace, his presence. None of us wants to live this way, hardened. And every heart, no matter how hard, has a small crack in it, waiting to crumble in the hands of our loving Father.

Jesus spoke reality to the disciples' fear. He basically said, "I'm just a few inches away." Jesus calmed their fear by letting them know they were not alone.

Jesus brings reality to our lives and fears as well. When we place our trust in Jesus, his reality sets us on solid ground and says, "It will be fine." We take the leap and move forward when we live in his truth and his reality. He reminds us: "Take courage, it is I; do not be afraid" (Mt 14:27). Let Jesus reign in your heart.

This process begins at our baptism, where we are claimed by Christ. We become God's sons and daughters. The mark of Baptism remains on our soul forever. By the grace of this sacrament, God abounds in our hearts, and the more we give him permission to take over, the more we experience his presence.

Jesus, too, was baptized. He approached John at the Jordan River to be plunged in the waters. Although Jesus didn't need to be baptized, he models this saving action for us. We all need to be cleansed of original sin and given the strength to withstand temptation. In Baptism we die to our sin, drowning in the holy waters, and are raised to new life in Christ. The mark of Christ is forever on our souls through the sacrament of Baptism.

The story of Jesus walking on water and Peter going out to meet him can be seen as an image of baptism. Being plunged in the water. Being saved by God, claimed as his child and living a life of surrender and trust.

Peter the Apostle said, "Lord, if it is you, command me to come to you on the water" (Mt 14:28). Jesus replied, "Come" (Mt 14:29). In this moment, Jesus asked Peter to step out of his fear and to trust him. Peter trusts and "begins" to walk on the water. Jesus asks us, too, to "come," to step out of the boat and to trust in him.

What's preventing you from jumping? Is fear keeping you from experiencing the fullness of life? Is it control? Is it hurt? Is it apathy? Name it and leave it behind as you jump into a new life with Christ. Claim victory, with God, over your fear, and trust in Jesus. Let him reign in your heart.

Just as we often do, Peter took his eyes off Jesus and got distracted by the storm. Peter began to *sink*. We all know that feeling—the stress, and the feeling that life is out of control. Jesus reached past the five or six inches of Peter's fear and caught him, pulling him up to safety. So, too, does Jesus approach us as we step out in our fear.

Life will always have obstacles. Storms will always come and go. To experience no pain, failure, or problems is impossible. But what keeps us from sinking is the confidence that in the midst of it all, God remains. He remains faithful. He remains steady. He remains in the waters of life with us. And when we put our trust in him, he always catches us.

We, by our own merit, cannot jump in the deep end or walk on water. But with God's help, we can. With him, we can make it through any circumstance. "Trust in the LORD with all your heart, on your own intelligence do not rely; in all your ways be mindful of him, and he will make straight your paths" (Prv 3:5–6). God's grace moves us, helping us to gain traction so we can live in authentic freedom: "I have the strength for everything through him who empowers me" (Phil 4:13).

As we face our fears, excuses, regrets, and worries, as we surrender and trust in God, and as our relationship with God grows, we, too, grow and move forward.

"I for my part do not consider myself to have taken possession. Just one thing: forgetting what lies behind but straining forward to what lies ahead, I continue my pursuit toward the goal, the prize of God's upward calling, in Christ Jesus" (Phil 3:13–14). Here, St. Paul encourages us to look ahead, to "forget what lies behind," and to move forward in our lives.

St. Paul speaks of a "goal" and a "prize." What's the goal and what's the prize? The goal for you and me is to gain traction in our lives, living each day pursuing our ultimate destination: heaven. The prize is being in relationship with Christ and knowing that he is with us on our journey, every step. We are never alone. Christ is always with us.

The first year I played high school football was a joke. I didn't stand a chance of playing in a game, but my coach thought it was a good idea to have all the freshmen be a part of the team. This required us to practice every day and to dress in full uniform for the Friday night games. The games were fun, but my uniform never had to be washed that season. As freshmen, my friend and I were not going to play, so we spent most of our time on the sidelines joking around, waving to the cheerleaders and our friends in the stands. It was just fun to be a part of the team and have no responsibilities.

One game I was joking with my friend on the sidelines as usual. We were putting our football helmets on backward. We weren't paying attention and didn't realize that our team was losing badly, and our coach was upset. By the fourth quarter, he had had enough and began to put in backup players, taking out the starters. That's when my nightmare began.

I was standing way in the back, behind the other players, when the coach yelled, "George, get in the game!" Excited, my friend hit the top of my helmet, which was sitting backward on top of my head, ramming it down over my forehead. I was pushed through the crowd of players and was suddenly standing in front of the coach with my helmet stuck backward. To say he was angry would be an understatement. I was hoping he'd send me back to the bench, but he pushed me onto the field. For my first play in high school, I entered the huddle with my helmet on backward.

It's a scene I'll never forget, not only because it was funny and embarrassing but also because of how it felt to be unprepared for the moment.

I was the quarterback. I was wearing the uniform, I was at the game, but I was not prepared. I ran my first-ever play with my helmet on backward. Like I said, it was a nightmare.

God doesn't want us to stand on the sidelines, watching others play in the game, unprepared for the life he has in store for us. He wants us in the game. When St. Paul speaks about "straining forward to what lies ahead" (Phil 3:13), he's talking about being active, engaged, and prepared for life. Happiness isn't found by chance. Winning the lottery doesn't make you or me happy. True, authentic happiness comes from being actively engaged in the life God has for us. Fulfillment happens when we live with a purpose, knowing that God has a plan for our lives, and we can play an active role in that plan.

Intentions are only as good as the decisions that determine the direction our life goes. The prize, Christ, is the one who helps us move forward from our former way of life. His grace moves us forward in our decisions, helping us land at the destination he intends for us.

If I have the intention of losing weight but never exercise or eat healthy, then my intention accomplishes nothing. But if I take care of my body, my intention becomes active, ultimately helping me to be slimmer and healthier.

We all have good intentions, but are we willing to allow Christ to move us forward in each decision we make so that we can land at our ultimate destination, happiness with him?

St. Paul knew well what it meant to change and to find true happiness. He persecuted and executed Christians. Yet even he, a sinner, met Christ on the road to Damascus. Jesus gave him new lenses and a new vision for his life. The power of Christ, his Holy Spirit, actively moved Paul to change.

It's interesting that in Paul's conversion story God changed his name from Saul to Paul. God pursued Saul and gave him a new identity. The same is true for us. God pursues us and gives us a new identity in Christ. Paul knew what it meant to be made new. To find meaning. To find authentic happiness. Paul states, "Whoever is in Christ is a new creation: the old things have passed away; behold, new things have come" (2 Cor 5:17). We are made new in Christ. The old has passed away. Behold, only new things are ahead for us. Paul leaped off the edge of the diving board into a new life with Christ.

Each day we are moved to the edge of the board. And by God's grace, we leap. This reality is where we find true fulfillment and happiness—leaping into the life that God has for us.

REFLECTION QUESTIONS

1. When have you struggled with fear? Explain.
2. How has fear kept you from moving forward in your life?
3. How is God asking you to take the leap in your life?
4. Where do you feel God tugging you to do more, to serve, love, etc.?
5. When do you most often take your eyes off of Jesus?
6. How is God asking you to trust in him and to take courage?

CHAPTER 10

LIVE THE ABUNDANT LIFE

My first job after college was overseeing a youth outreach program at a church in my hometown. It was full-time work and part-time pay, but I loved it. My first day on the job involved organizing a large end-of-summer, back-to-school bash for the teenagers. This was my first real introduction to working with kids and, to some extent, parents. The event was "organized chaos" with different outdoor activities on the field next to the church. We had food and music. It was fun until I heard, "Oh my God! She's dead, I killed her!" I ran as fast as I could to the scene.

One of the male volunteers, a college-aged kid, was leading an intense game of sharks and minnows (a fast-paced game of tag) on one end of the field. This volunteer was a large guy—short and very stubby, weighing around three hundred pounds. Although he was hefty, he could apparently run really fast—in short spurts. And in doing so, he got caught up in the game and ran over a young high school girl at full speed. She stood about five feet tall and weighed no more than one hundred pounds. The impact was damaging.

When I arrived, kids were circled around her as she lay on the ground, out cold. She was alive and breathing but unconscious. My big volunteer guy was crying and yelling, "Is she going to be OK?" By the time the ambulance arrived, she was sitting up and talking. At the hospital the doctors told us she suffered a mild concussion, whiplash, and bruising. In the doctor's words, "It's basically like she got in a car wreck, but she'll be fine." I still can't believe I didn't lose my job.

Later I drove the big volunteer guy home. He was still shaken up. I told him to calm down and then asked him what happened.

"I was running so fast that I didn't see her, and before I knew it, I ran right over her," he said.

"Why so fast with kids smaller than you?" I asked.

"I just got caught up in the game and forgot about everything else."

"Yes," I said, jokingly. "And you almost killed a kid doing so!"

I'm guilty of this—running at a pace I'm not meant for. I'm guilty of thinking that my fast pace is productive and that my productivity affirms my identity. Busy means I'm important. We all get caught up in the game of life and move at a pace we aren't created for, all the while running over things, even people. We often neglect things and forget what's important, missing out on the beautiful parts of life. What's the rush?

Some people move so fast that they just spin their wheels and go nowhere. They have no traction. The treads on their tires are mostly worn off. Why do we move so fast?

God wants us to live a life of abundance, not chaos! And the abundant life is not found in the rapid game of sharks and minnows but in living at the pace for which he created us.

"I came so that they might have life and have it more abundantly," Jesus said (Jn 10:10). This is what you and I are intended for: a life of freedom, of joy, of abundance. This is the life we long for and the one we have been discussing in this book. But what does Jesus mean by "abundant" life?

When we hear the word *abundant*, we might think about "things" or "stuff." Whether we are rich, poor, or in-between, Jesus does not mean that things will make us happy. An abundant life is not a life of storing up earthly treasures. God wants much more for us than things. He wants us to have an abundance of himself. He wants us to share in his life. He wants to shower us with his grace and love. The abundant life is a life in relationship with Jesus, where he guides us in everything we do. And Jesus freely offers us this life, every day.

Just before speaking about abundant life, Jesus says, "A thief comes only to steal and slaughter and destroy" (Jn 10:10). So much in the world and in our lives is waiting to steal our joy, peace, and freedom. There is no greater work of the enemy than keeping us busy and focused on the things that don't bring us abundant life.

My friend Ennie has a motto, "Grab a rocking chair and sit on the front porch." Slow down, relax, and enjoy life, the way God intended. This doesn't mean we neglect work or family responsibilities. Rather, we put life in perspective, and live at the pace we are created for—a pace at which we can notice other people, a pace that allows us to live in God's embrace. A pace that makes us available to love others. A pace at which we stop running away from reality. A pace that reminds us our identity isn't wrapped in what we do, but in who we are. A pace that gives us time to think. A pace that frees us to volunteer and serve, a pace at which we can breathe, deeply.

Years ago I received a frantic call from a friend. At age thirty-two he was experiencing a heart condition. His heart was off rhythm. He asked me to be with him and his wife as he prepared for open-heart surgery. It was scary. When I arrived, the doctor was talking with them.

"OK," the doctor said, "I'll just be honest with you. We are going to put you to sleep, crack your chest open, and grab your heart." We were all staring at the doctor, holding back tears.

"Then we are going to stop your heart from beating, and for a moment today, you are going to die." At this point, tears were rolling down our faces. "Then we are going to 'kick' your heart back on, in hopes that it will beat on rhythm again."

Our hearts must beat to keep us alive, but if a heart beats off rhythm, at the wrong pace, it will eventually wear out.

The surgery was a success, and today my friend's heart beats at the right pace. His life slowed down that day. He actually died and came back to life with a new heartbeat, one that is on rhythm. The doctors slowed down his heart to change its pace.

God wants to reach into our hearts and lives, slow us down, and restart the way we do things so we can live at a new pace. He wants our hearts to beat in rhythm *with his*. He knows that when we walk in lockstep with him, we live in freedom, abundantly experiencing his love. And when we don't live in rhythm with him, the enemy is quick to try to steal space in our hearts, take over our pace, and push us to a speed where we lose perspective.

I know we live in a busy world. I understand the life of family, work, school, friends, bills, and chaos. I understand that our lives can be hectic. I also know that we can downsize our calendars and allow more time for what's essential.

It might sound counterintuitive, but in order to gain traction and move forward, we must slow down. Many of my conversations with people focus on balance and pace of life. In these talks people express the feeling that they can't juggle everything—work, family, marriage, finances, and so forth. Most people, myself included, admit that they get "caught up in the game" and, before they know it, are moving at a pace that is exhausting. Eventually they wear out. Often people throw up their hands and say, "I guess this is just how life is supposed to be." I even have people tell me, "I'll rest when I die." Wow, what a sad outlook. All the while, their busyness keeps their lives scattered and unprioritized. Maybe, from the outside, they look "successful." But happy? No.

Were we created to live so fast? Can we begin to slow down and experience the abundant life God has for us?

When my wife, Gretchen, and I were dating, about to become engaged, a mentor couple told us to begin scheduling date nights once a week. We thought it was a good idea, but we had flexible schedules and lots of free time to spend together—we didn't really need proper "dates" back then. But this couple insisted that if we committed to scheduling time together then, we would have a routine in place when life became hectic. So we did, and whew! Were they right!

Once jobs got bigger and kids came into the picture, we had less time for our relationship. But we had disciplined ourselves to schedule time together, no matter what life looked like. When life is busy and our pace becomes too hectic, we still make time for our marriage.

Everyone agrees that in order to have a thriving marriage, you must spend time together, communicate well, and grow in knowledge of each other. Intimacy is key to a strong relationship, and sharing time with each other builds intimacy. If you want a marriage that is abundant, spend time together.

A friend once said to me that the word *intimacy* means, "into me see." Intimacy is being able to see into the other's heart. Imagine a marriage or any close friendship in which two people are always apart and don't communicate regularly. How strong or deep would that relationship be?

Gretchen and I have noticed that when our relationship struggles, we can usually point to lack of time and communication. When we become too busy to give attention to each other and to communicate, tension builds—because we don't feel as if we are a priority in each other's life.

Love grows as we invest in each other. Time, attention, and communication remind us how much we love each other. When we don't invest in one another, we withdraw money from our account without depositing any. Over time, we run out. Then what?

It's the same in our relationship with God. We need to slow our pace and spend time communicating with him. The abundant life is a life in which we invest our time in knowing God and letting God know us. This is called prayer. Prayer has a unique way of slowing the pace of our lives and putting our perspective in right order. In prayer, we fall in love again, fear decreases, we trust in the future. In prayer, we let go of the past, we come to know God intimately, and he comes to know us. Our relationship thrives. In prayer, God slows us down, puts treads on our tires, and helps us gain the traction we need to move forward in life.

When my marriage begins to lack peace and joy, it is usually because I'm not investing time with Gretchen. Likewise, when my spiritual or interior life is lacking, I'm not investing time with God.

No time, no peace.

Anything important to us requires time. If you want to find out what's important to me, look at my calendar, and you will see how I invest my time. What does your calendar look like? There was a time when I said I had certain priorities, but my calendar said otherwise. I had to make a shift, a change in my rhythm. My priorities of faith, family, friends, work, and leisure had to show on my calendar if they were to materialize in my daily life.

Imagine your spouse or your best friend telling you that you need to work on having a better relationship. And your response is, "I just don't have time." What would be your spouse's or best friend's reaction? Your answer is telling them that they aren't a priority in your life.

Time is a four-letter word that speaks of another four-letter word—*love*. A mentor once told me that your kids will spell love like this: T-I-M-E. I have seen the wisdom of this simple statement in my own life. I've seen both sides of investing and not investing time in people who are important to me.

If you, like me, have not always invested time in what really matters in life, don't be discouraged. As we gain perspective, we can, with God's help, reprioritize and spend time where it's most important. We can never get time back, but we can start now to invest properly to live a life of happiness.

The same can be said in our relationship with God. We must carve out space in our lives to talk with God. Jesus taught us how to pray. Scripture shows us that throughout his earthly ministry, Jesus would retreat to pray, to spend time with God. The Gospel of Luke says, "But he would withdraw to deserted places to pray" (Lk 5:16).

Jesus invites us to do the same—to spend time reflecting and plugging into the source of happiness, God. Jesus said, "But when you pray, go to your inner room, close the door, and pray to your Father" (Mt 6:6).

Silence is essential to our joy. We must have some quiet time, reflecting and praying to the Father. In this hectic world, loud and busy, it is crucial to our happiness that we unplug for a while, and plug into God. Don't be afraid to carve out space in your day to chat with God. Let your calendar show what you love.

I often hear this statement from people: "I don't know how to pray." Prayer can seem complicated, a mystery that only saints have figured out. I remember thinking this as well. How do I pray? How can I get to know God better?

A good place to start is to consider two things I'm sure you've already mastered—talking and listening. These are the only tools you need to communicate with God. Talk and listen. Sometimes listening is the more important (and the more difficult) part.

I'm not sure there is a perfect formula for prayer, but I know prayer is a must. We need to make time to speak to God and to listen to his voice. There are many books that give great insight into prayer. There are different forms and styles of prayer. The Church is full of wonderful saints who teach us how to pray. Scripture, God's word, is both a source of prayer and inspiration for prayer. Reflection and meditation can be effective forms of prayer. But if you just take time to talk and listen to God, you will receive abundant fruit.

Your life and mine are different, better, happier, more abundant, when we spend time with God.

My friend Matt Maher, who wrote the foreword for this book, wrote a beautiful song called "Alive Again." It's based on a prayer from St. Augustine of Hippo, one of the early Fathers of the Church. Augustine's prayer conveys the intimacy of talking to God from the heart, and shows how authentic prayer allows us to come alive again.

Late have I loved you, O Beauty ever ancient, ever new. Late have I loved you! You were within me, but I was outside, and it was there that I searched for you. In my unloveliness I plunged into the lovely things which you created. You were with me, but I was not with you. Created things kept me from you; yet if they had not been in you, they would have not been at all. You called, you shouted, and you broke through my deafness. You flashed, you shone, and you dispelled my blindness. You breathed your fragrance on me; I drew in breath and now I pant for you. I have tasted you, now I hunger and thirst for more. You touched me, and I burned for your peace.[1]

Augustine's prayer is amazing to me. It's honest and real. He understood the human condition. We fail, we run, we are late, we are busy, we get lost, and we get stuck on the diving board, yet God remains faithful.

To understand this prayer from St. Augustine, it's important to know his story. Augustine lived life at a rapid pace, far from God. He was a pagan. He was well educated and successful, yet morally immature, living a worldly life of lust. Augustine had an abundance of "things," but he didn't have the abundant life. His mother, Monica, prayed for his conversion to Christ. Monica believed that it's never too late and we are never too far away for God to reach us.

Augustine wrestled with leaving his sinful life. He wanted authentic happiness, but he found superficial consolation in things of the flesh. Ultimately, his questions about God and finding true happiness led him to a total turnaround, a drastic conversion. He found the source of happiness, God, and left behind his old ways of living. Today, Augustine is known as one of the great Fathers of the Church and a saint. He was far from God, but Augustine knew that God never gave up on him, that God would rescue him.

God never gives up on us either, no matter how frantic our pace. He calls, he shouts, and he breaks through our deafness. And we say, "You touched me, and I burned for your peace."[2]

God wants to break through our lives, our deafness. He longs to have a relationship with us—through prayer—so that we can live in rhythm with him. The *Catechism* describes it this way:

> *God calls man first.* Man may forget his Creator or hide far from his face; he may run after idols or accuse the deity of having abandoned him; yet the living and true God tirelessly calls each person to that mysterious encounter known as prayer. In prayer, the faithful God's initiative of love always comes first; our own first step is always a response. As God gradually reveals himself and reveals man to himself, prayer appears as a reciprocal call, a covenant drama. Through words and actions, this drama engages the heart. It unfolds throughout the whole history of salvation. (*CCC*, 2567)

My mom is one of my biggest cheerleaders. Since I can remember, she was, and still is, always encouraging me. Her encouragement in anxious moments often reminded me that I could do something I feared. But as good as my mom's words are, and as important as her encouragement is, no words speak truth to our hearts more than God's. His word is truth—always. (You might pause here to consider how you value words from your family, friends, and spouse. How does this compare to the value you place on God's communication?) This is why praying regularly and reading scripture is vital to our souls. God's words, which we hear through prayer, remind us of who we are and who we are not.

Prayer also reminds us that we are forgiven, allowing space for us to ask for mercy, giving us permission to leave things in the past. We are no longer defined by our mistakes but by God's definition of us as his son or daughter. The abundant life fundamentally involves understanding and knowing God's mercy and forgiveness. In prayer we become aware of our faults, weaknesses, and brokenness. God helps us figure out why we do what we do, so that we can change what we need to change.

One of the great joys of being Catholic is the grace of the sacraments—visible signs of God's actual grace and presence. The sacrament of Reconciliation, or confession, is one particularly fruitful way to experience the mercy and forgiveness of God. The abundant life is lived by the grace of this sacrament.

Finally, the abundant life is a life that is lived with purpose. When we grasp God's love for us and know our identity as his sons and daughters, we are changed. Our new life, the abundant life in Christ, moves us to love, abundantly. In the sacraments of Baptism and Confirmation, and through prayer, we receive the power of Christ living in us. His life in us is the Holy Spirit. God's Spirit is moving and active in our lives, moving us to love. In scripture we see God pouring out his Spirit (Acts 1:8).

The *Catechism* says, "On the day of Pentecost when the seven weeks of Easter had come to an end, Christ's Passover is fulfilled in the outpouring of the Holy Spirit, manifested, given, and communicated as a divine person: of his fullness, Christ, the Lord, pours out the Spirit in abundance" (*CCC*, 731). We, too, receive the abundance of Christ's Spirit.

Through God's Spirit, we are moved to love and to take action in the world.

Fr. Raniero Cantalamessa, preacher to the papal household, quotes Ignatius of Latakia in one of his homilies:

> Without the Holy Spirit: God is far away, Christ stays in the past, the Gospel is a dead letter, the Church is simply an organization, authority a matter of domination, mission a matter of propaganda, liturgy no more than an evocation, Christian living a slave morality. But with the Holy Spirit: the cosmos is resurrected and groans with the birth-pangs of the Kingdom, the risen Christ is there, the Gospel is the power of life, the Church shows forth the life of the Trinity, authority is a liberating service, mission is a Pentecost, the liturgy is both memorial and anticipation, human action is deified.[3]

The power of the Holy Spirit moved the apostles and believers of the Early Church to change the world. We, too, are called to live that life. We may not travel the world, speak to large audiences, write books, or be known; but we can love others with the power of Christ. We can use our small gifts by offering them to our families, friends, neighbors, and local churches. Together we can make a difference and be world changers.

St. Paul said to Timothy, "For God did not give us a spirit of cowardice but rather of power and love and self-control" (2 Tm 1:7). The abundance of God lives in us and moves us past our fears. We are moved to action. When we live fully in Christ, we live with a purpose to be difference makers in the world. Look around you. I'm sure you won't have to look far to find someone to love or some place to serve. God is calling you. Let him move you to love, to live abundantly, and to live with purpose. Mother Teresa said to start by loving those "within a ten-foot radius of you." That's the best place to begin. Right where you are.

Marianne Williamson describes the power of living with purpose:

> Our deepest fear is not that we are inadequate. Our deepest fear is that we are powerful beyond measure. It is our light, not our darkness, that most frightens us. We ask ourselves, Who am I to be brilliant, gorgeous, talented, fabulous? Actually, who are you not to be? You are a child of God. Your playing small does not serve the world. There is nothing enlightened about shrinking so that other people won't feel insecure around you. We are all meant to shine, as children do. We were born to make manifest the glory of God that is within us. It's not just in some of us; it's in everyone. And as we let our own light shine, we unconsciously give other people permission to do the same. As we are liberated from our own fear, our presence automatically liberates others.[4]

In Christ we find liberation from our fears and become who God created us to be. Cardinal Oscar Rodríguez taught me that after basic needs are met, there isn't much difference between those with a ton of money and those with little. Those who are happy are those who are generous. True poverty is being spiritually bankrupt, not living an authentic life in Christ. Your time of spiritual bankruptcy is over. Your time to live the abundant life in Christ is now. Create space in your heart for God and ask Jesus to dwell there.

Do you want an authentic life, a life of happiness, a full life at a slower pace, in rhythm with your Creator? God is calling you, loudly. He is searching for you in the garden, running to meet you when you turn toward him, reaching for you, inches away from your grasp, as your toes curl around the end of the diving board. Jump! He will catch you, and your life will never be the same.

Live the abundant life with Christ, each day. Pope Benedict XVI says, "Do not be afraid of Christ! He takes nothing away, and he gives you everything. When we give ourselves to him, we receive a hundredfold in return."[5]

Turn from the counterfeit to the authentic. Rethink your life. Simply turn toward God and ask him to carry you through life.

He wants you. He longs for you. He loves you.

He is authentic happiness.

REFLECTION QUESTIONS

1. In what ways do you find that you live at a pace that is too fast?
2. How does God want you to slow down so you can experience the life he has for you?
3. Where do you need your heart, your life, to beat in rhythm with God?
4. What areas of your life do you need to stop and enjoy more?
5. How can you begin to make prayer a priority in your life?
6. How can you engage more in the sacramental life of the Church?
7. Where do you need the Holy Spirit to empower you in your life?

ACKNOWLEDGMENTS

Gretchen, I am forever grateful to God for you and the gift you are to me, and our family. You have taught me so many things—to have joy, to overcome fear, to live in hope—but the greatest has been the ability to love. Thank you for all your love and sacrifices and for bringing such joy to my life.

Marie, I never experienced having a father's heart until you came into the world. Thank you for making it so easy to love, for loving me and accepting me as a dad, a dad who is still learning every day. I'm so proud of you, your faith, and your passion for life. Geaux get 'em! I love you, Ria.

Jacob, I'm so proud to be your dad. Watching you grow into a young man has been such a joy for me, especially seeing your faith blossom. I can't thank you enough for teaching me how to see the world and live my faith in it. And to have courage. You are my champ. I love you, Jakes.

Sarah, you bring me so much joy. I can't imagine life without your smile. Your love for life and your passion for people will change the world. You have taught me how to live in ways I never would have tried. I can't thank you enough for your unconditional love. I love you, Bell.

Clare, I was the first to hold you in the middle of the night while your mom was in emergency surgery. From the very beginning, you stole my heart. Our family is better because of you. Your faith and joy for life give me hope for a world in need of them. I love you, Clare Therese.

Adeline, your life has transformed all of us. You are a gift to our family and to the world. Most important, you have taught me that God's plans are far greater than my own. I can't wait to see what great things God does in your life. I love you, Addie.

Mom, thank you for teaching me to follow my dreams and for leading the way by reaching your own. Thank you for always believing in me, encouraging me, and loving me, even when it was tough. Thank you for giving me life and for motivating me to live it to the full. Thank you for helping me with this project. You inspire me, Mom, and I love you!

Dad, I love you. I'm blessed to say that I never doubted whether my dad loved me. Thank you for always being there, always loving me, always supporting me, and always believing in me. You taught me so many things, but teaching me how to love my kids through the way you loved and still love me is the best one.

Lulie, you are the best big sister in the world. You may have driven me to countless games and sat in the stands cheering me on (thank you, by the way), but truth be told, I'm *your* greatest fan. I love watching you live life with such joy. You are an amazing wife, mother, sister, and friend.

To my family and friends—the list is too long, and for that I am a blessed man. Thanks to all of you. You know who you are, and I love you.

Special thanks to Matt for writing the foreword to this book. Love you, brother.

To our communities, from Arizona to Georgia to Louisiana. Community has kept us going and encouraged us to trust in God's plan. Thank you.

To Ave Maria Press, and especially Kristi McDonald—thanks for reaching out and making this possible.

NOTES

1. We Are All Starving

1. Alfred Delp, *Alfred Delp, S.J.: Prison Writings* (1958; Maryknoll, NY: Orbis, 2004).

2. It's Time to Surrender

1. Joseph Ratzinger, "The New Evangelization: Building the Civilization of Love," Address to Catechists and Religion Teachers, Jubilee of Catechists, December 12, 2000.

2. Maxwell Anderson, *Joan of Lorraine: A Play in Two Acts* (1946), act 2, scene 3.

3. Thomas Aquinas, *Summa Theologiæ*, II-II, Q. 29, Art. 2.

4. Anselm is credited with the phrase "faith seeking understanding." It was the original title of his *Proslogion*.

5. John Paul II, *Faith and Reason* (cf. Ex 33:18; Pss 27:8–9, 63:2–3; Jn 14:8; 1 Jn 3:2).

6. Vincent Arong, "What Is a Mystery?" http://www.biblicalcatholic.com/apologetics/p8.htm.

3. Rethink Happiness

1. Bishop Richard Challoner, *Think Well On't* (1728), now available as *Think Well On It: Considerations on the Great Truths of the Catholic Religion* (Charlotte, NC: Tan Books, 2009).

2. St. Augustine, *The Confessions of St. Augustine*, bk. 1, chap. 1.

3. Ratzinger, "The New Evangelization," December 12, 2000.

5. Keep It Real

1. John Paul II, Apostolic Journey to the United States of America, Mass at the Boston Common: Homily (October 1, 1979), website of the Holy See.

2. John Paul II, Apostolic Visit to Toronto, Mass for the Celebration of the 17th World Youth Day in Downsview Park, Toronto: Homily (July 28, 2002), website of the Holy See.

6. Recover What Was Lost

1. Ratzinger, "The New Evangelization," December 12, 2000.

2. https://adoreministries.com.

7. Recognize Authentic Beauty

1. Sharon Jayson, "Generation Y's Goal? Wealth and Fame," *USA Today*, updated January 10, 2007, http://usatoday30.usatoday.com/news/nation/2007-01-09-gen-y-cover_x.htm.

2. "The Family She Founded," Mother Teresa of Calcutta website, http://www.motherteresa.org/07_family/family00.html.

3. Dorothy S. Hunt, ed., *Love: A Fruit Always in Season— Daily Meditations by Mother Teresa* (San Francisco: Ignatius Press, 1987), 129.

8. See with New Lenses

1. As quoted in *Mother Teresa's Reaching Out In Love: Stories Told by Mother Teresa*, comp. and ed. Edward Le Joly and Jaya Chaliha (New York: Barnes and Noble, 2002), 122.

9. Take the Leap

1. John Paul II, Mass at the Beginning of the Pontificate: Homily (October 22, 1978), website of the Holy See.

2. John Paul II, Apostolic Visit to Toronto, to Ciudad de Guatemala and to Ciudad de Mexico, 17th World Youth Day, Papal Welcoming Ceremony (July 25, 2002), website of the Holy See.

10. Live the Abundant Life

1. St. Augustine, *Confessions*, bk. 10, chap. 27.

2. St. Augustine, *Confessions*, bk. 10, chap. 27.

3. Fr. Raniero Cantalamessa, *Mary: Mirror of the Church*, trans. Frances Lonergan Villa (Collegeville, MN: Liturgical Press, 1992), 151.

4. Marianne Williamson, *A Return to Love: Reflections on the Principles of "A Course on Miracles"* (New York: HarperCollins, 1992), 191.

5.   Benedict XVI, Mass for the Inauguration of the Pontificate: Homily (April 24, 2005), website of the Holy See.

Paul George is a Catholic speaker, teacher, and author who cofounded Adore Ministries and served as its president for eight years. He has more than twenty years of ministry experience as a parish youth minister, diocesan director, campus minister, and full-time evangelist. George is a life coach and, through his organization Art of Living, serves as a consultant to churches, schools, organizations, and corporations throughout the world. George is the host of a national radio show and podcast, *The Paul George Show*. He is a speaker at Steubenville conferences and spoke at World Youth Day in both Rome and Australia.

George earned his bachelor's degree from Louisiana College in 1997 and his master's degree in theological studies from the University of Dallas in 2008. He has served as national director of Life Teen International and a professor of theology at the Aquinas Institute. He wrote several Bible studies, including *The Art of Living*, *Let's Be Honest*, and *What If*. He also authored both a student's guide and a teacher's guide to the new YOUCAT.

George and his wife, Gretchen, live in Lafayette, Louisiana, with their children.

www.paulgeorge.la
Twitter, Instagram: @paulgeorgeii

AVE

AVE MARIA PRESS

Founded in 1865, Ave Maria Press,
a ministry of the Congregation of
Holy Cross, is a Catholic publishing
company that serves the spiritual and
formative needs of the Church and its
schools, institutions, and ministers;
Christian individuals and families; and
others seeking spiritual nourishment.

For a complete listing of titles from

Ave Maria Press

Sorin Books

Forest of Peace

Christian Classics

visit www.avemariapress.com

AVE MARIA PRESS
Notre Dame, IN
A Ministry of the United States Province of Holy Cross